JOHN ST

Utilitarianism

With Related Remarks from Mill's Other Writings

JOHN STUART MILL

Utilitarianism

With Related Remarks from Mill's Other Writings

Edited, with an Introduction, by Ben Eggleston

Hackett Publishing Company, Inc.
Indianapolis/Cambridge

For further information, please address
   Hackett Publishing Company, Inc.
   P.O. Box 44937
   Indianapolis, Indiana 46244-0937

   www.hackettpublishing.com

Cover design by Brian Rak
Interior design by Elizabeth L. Wilson
Composition by Aptara, Inc.

Library of Congress Cataloging-in-Publication Data

Names: Mill, John Stuart, 1806–1873, author. | Eggleston, Ben, 1971– editor.
Title: Utilitarianism : with related remarks from Mill's other writings / John Stuart
   Mill ; edited by Ben Eggleston.
Description: Indianapolis : Hackett Publishing Company, Inc., 2017. | Includes
   bibliographical references.
Identifiers: LCCN 2016038761| ISBN 9781624665455 (pbk.) | ISBN
   9781624665462 (cloth)
Subjects: LCSH: Utilitarianism. | Mill, John Stuart, 1806–1873. Utilitarianism.
Classification: LCC B1603 .U87 2017 | DDC 171/.5—dc23
LC record available at https://lccn.loc.gov/2016038761

Acknowledgments

Like virtually all recent researchers into the thought of John Stuart Mill, I am indebted to John M. Robson and the other scholars who assembled the *Collected Works of John Stuart Mill* (thirty-three volumes, University of Toronto Press, 1963–1991). Enormously ambitious and meticulously executed, this project revolutionized access to Mill's writings. In addition, the Liberty Fund, Inc., has performed a great service by making the *Collected Works* available on its website.

More particularly, I am indebted to the following authors and their works for their illuminating scholarship on Mill's moral philosophy and for bringing to my attention many passages from Mill's writings that are usefully read alongside Mill's *Utilitarianism*:

- Fred Berger, *Happiness, Justice, and Freedom: The Moral and Political Philosophy of John Stuart Mill* (University of California Press, 1984)

- Roger Crisp, *Mill on Utilitarianism* (Routledge, 1997)

- Roger Crisp, introductory material and notes in his edition of Mill's *Utilitarianism* (Oxford University Press, 1998)

- Dale E. Miller, endnotes and commentary in *The Basic Writings of John Stuart Mill: On Liberty, The Subjection of Women, and Utilitarianism* (Random House, 2002)

- Henry R. West, *An Introduction to Mill's Utilitarian Ethics* (Cambridge University Press, 2004)

- Henry R. West, *Mill's Utilitarianism: A Reader's Guide* (Continuum, 2007)

- Dale E. Miller, *J. S. Mill: Moral, Social and Political Thought* (Polity, 2010)

- David O. Brink, *Mill's Progressive Principles* (Oxford University Press, 2013)

I have also learned much from the Mill scholarship of D. G. Brown, Wendy Donner, Daniel Jacobson, and Jonathan Riley.

For helpful feedback on a draft of this volume, I wish to thank David Brink, Roger Crisp, Dale Dorsey, and John Skorupski. I also benefited from the support of Piers Norris Turner and Henry West, who provided favorable referee reports to Hackett (and revealed their identities to me).

My greatest debt is to Dale Miller, with whom I have been discussing forms of utilitarianism, including Mill's, since we were in graduate school in the 1990s. Dale's knowledge of Mill has always greatly surpassed mine, and my work on Mill has always benefited from his expertise. The present volume is no exception: his close reading and judicious advice led to major improvements, for which I am very grateful.

Contents

Contents

Part 1:

About This Book

Mill's *Utilitarianism*

John Stuart Mill's *Utilitarianism* is one of the most important works in the history of moral philosophy. Though just a fraction of the size of most philosophy books (both of Mill's time and ours), it provides a rich articulation and defense of an influential approach to thinking about ethics.

Mill lived in England, from 1806 to 1873. Although the nineteenth century was a time of great progress in England, Mill found the moral thought prevalent in his society to rely too much on tradition, the uncritical acceptance of existing practices, and facile appeals to intuition. Rejecting these ideas, he was drawn to an approach to morality that grounded it on the promotion of happiness—the approach he would later call "utilitarianism." In the first part of the nineteenth century, the best-known formulations of this approach were William Paley's *The Principles of Moral and Political Philosophy* (1785) and Jeremy Bentham's *An Introduction to the Principles of Morals and Legislation* (1789). But Mill felt that these works contained some defects that blighted the forms of utilitarianism they propounded; he wanted to do better. These circumstances formed the background for his own foray into a systematic presentation of utilitarian thinking.

Mill's *Utilitarianism* was first published as a series of three magazine articles in 1861, and as a book in 1863. Although utilitarian ideas have subsequently found expression in the works of writers ranging from Mill's near-contemporary Henry Sidgwick to twenty-first-century philosophers such as Peter Singer, Mill's essay is probably more widely read by today's students and scholars than any other utilitarian work. It might well be the single most widely read work in moral philosophy generally. The reasons for this influence are not hard to surmise. As mentioned above, the book is short. (Mill knew this would help; he wrote to a friend, "small books are so much more read than large ones that it is an advantage when one's matter will go into a small space" [*Collected Works* vol. XV, p. 645].) The writing is eloquent and animated, and Mill's insights and argumentation are penetrating, by the standards of any era. Finally, whether due to good judgment or just good luck on the part of Mill, many of the topics that he explores in depth in *Utilitarianism*—such as the nature of happiness, the role of rules in morality, and the compatibility of justice with promoting overall good—are ones that especially interest today's readers.

Why Read *Utilitarianism*
with Related Remarks?

Although Mill probably intended *Utilitarianism* to be the clearest and most complete statement of his moral philosophy, he was so prolific a writer—both as a specialized philosopher and as a public intellectual—that his other works inevitably include remarks that reflect his utilitarian commitments. Mill wrote long essays with substantial ethical content both before and after *Utilitarianism*, and even his works in other areas of philosophy contain a number of remarks that seem to evince his utilitarianism.

The related remarks included in this edition are diverse, but many of them fall into a few basic categories. Some restate or amplify key claims of *Utilitarianism*. Some comment on specific passages in *Utilitarianism* or helpfully elaborate on topics dispatched briefly in *Utilitarianism*. And some provide discussions of specific aspects of Mill's moral thought that would not have been out of place in *Utilitarianism*, had Mill chosen to include them there.

The reasons for reading *Utilitarianism* with these related remarks are twofold. First, ever since its publication, *Utilitarianism* has prompted its readers to ask questions that the text itself does not fully answer—questions about the precise content of Mill's views, or their implications, or Mill's reasons for holding them. Many of the related remarks included in this edition shed light on these topics.

Second, for most students and scholars, the point of reading Mill's *Utilitarianism* is to understand his utilitarianism: that is, to understand the moral theory he embraced after the extensive reading, writing, discussion, and reflection that we know his intellectual life comprised. This goal is as truly served by reading the related remarks as by reading *Utilitarianism* itself.

In reading the related remarks, two caveats must be kept in mind. First, by necessity for an edition of this kind, every remark (except for a diary entry) is taken out of context. In many cases, consulting the longer passage from which the remark is drawn will provide valuable perspective. (To facilitate this, a bibliographic citation accompanies every remark.) Second, the related remarks do not necessarily clarify or expand on the meaning of Mill's *Utilitarianism*. All one can be sure of is that they are parts of Mill's utilitarianism. Like all prolific writers, Mill might express incompatible thoughts in various places, either by accident or due to a change of mind. Of course, such conflicts are of interest in their own right, especially for historians of philosophy.

How to Read This Edition of *Utilitarianism*

Part 2 of this edition includes the text of *Utilitarianism*, fifty-eight related remarks by Mill, and some explanatory and bibliographic insertions. In this edition, the text of *Utilitarianism* has been modified in the following ways.

In a marginal notation next to the first line of each paragraph, chapter and paragraph numbers are provided—for example, "IV.9" for Chapter IV, paragraph 9. This is because passages in *Utilitarianism* are often cited in this way.

There is one other common way of citing passages in *Utilitarianism*—namely, by reference to pages of volume X of the *Collected Works of John Stuart Mill*. Accordingly, those page numbers are inserted into the text, in brackets—for example, "[p. 215]."

The text of each chapter includes one or more superscripted numerals and is followed by corresponding endnotes. These endnotes present related remarks from works by Mill other than *Utilitarianism*. Everything in the endnotes is additional material—*Utilitarianism* itself has four footnotes (two in Chapter II and two in Chapter V), but no endnotes. Mill's footnotes are marked with asterisks, and the endnotes are marked with Arabic numerals, restarting at 1 after each chapter.

In the endnotes, the related remarks are preceded by introductory comments. These introductory comments are provided in a font without serifs—like this—in order to distinguish them from the related remarks, which are in the same font used for the text of *Utilitarianism* (and for most of Part 1 of this edition). In the related remarks, brackets are used to indicate the insertion of text, such as page numbers (as in the text of *Utilitarianism*), ellipses denoting elided text, or words of clarification (such as the referent of a pronoun used by Mill).

You could read all five chapters of *Utilitarianism*, and then turn to the endnotes. Or, while reading *Utilitarianism*, you could jump to each endnote exactly when signified in the text. I recommend an intermediate approach: reading a given chapter straight through, then reading the related remarks presented in that chapter's endnotes. The introductory comment for each endnote indicates the *Utilitarianism* paragraph to which it pertains, so that you don't have to go back and hunt around too much for the endnote numerals in the text of *Utilitarianism*.

After you read Chapter V and its endnotes, read the three appendices. Note that *Utilitarianism* itself has no appendices; the appendices in this edition are used to form groups of related remarks on three particular topics that are important to understanding *Utilitarianism*.

The Other Works by Mill Excerpted in This Edition

The related remarks that accompany the text of *Utilitarianism* in this edition are drawn from twenty-nine of Mill's other works. All of these works (and many others) are included in the *Collected Works of John Stuart Mill*, a monumental project of thirty-three volumes produced by the University of Toronto Press from 1963 to 1991. The *Collected Works* can be found in many university libraries. As of this writing the *Collected Works* is also available on the website of the Liberty Fund, Inc. (a private educational foundation).

On the next several pages is a table containing some information about the works from which the related remarks are drawn, along with additional information about *Utilitarianism* itself. The works are listed in chronological order of publication.

In each row, the first column gives the name of the work and its location in the *Collected Works* (CW). Locations are specified by volume number and page range.

The second column gives some background information about the work, such as the occasion of Mill's writing of it or the circumstances of its publication.

The third column indicates where the work is excerpted in the notes and appendices in this edition of *Utilitarianism*. Locations in notes are given by chapter number and note number. For example, the first row of the table below indicates that an excerpt from "Brodie's History of the British Empire" is provided in note 1 at the end of Chapter II. Locations in appendices are given by appendix letter (A, B, or C).

Work	Information	Location
"Brodie's History of the British Empire," CW vol. VI, pp. 1–58	In 1822, George Brodie, a Scottish historian, published *A History of the British Empire*. In 1824, Mill published a review of Brodie's book in the *Westminster Review*.	IIn1
"Remarks on Bentham's Philosophy," CW vol. X, pp. 3–18	As mentioned in this introduction (see "Mill's *Utilitarianism*"), Jeremy Bentham was an influential earlier utilitarian. In 1833, one year after Bentham's death, Mill wrote an essay on Bentham to aid the popular writer Edward Bulwer (now better known as Edward Bulwer-Lytton) in writing *England and the English*. Contrary to Mill's expectation (letter to Thomas Carlyle, 1833, CW vol. XII, p. 172), his entire essay was printed (in June 1833) as an appendix to Bulwer's book.	IIn1, IIIn1
"Blakey's History of Moral Science," CW vol. X, pp. 19–29	In 1833, Robert Blakey, an Irish philosopher, published *The History of Moral Science*. In October 1833, Mill published a review of Blakey's book in the *Monthly Repository*.	IIn11
Letter to Thomas Carlyle, CW vol. XII, pp. 204–9	Thomas Carlyle was a Scottish philosopher and historian. This letter is dated January 12, 1834.	IIn6
"Sedgwick's Discourse," CW vol. X, pp. 31–74	In 1833, Adam Sedgwick, a professor at the University of Cambridge, published *A Discourse on the Studies of the University of Cambridge*. In this book, he criticized utilitarianism, at least in the form in which it had been espoused in William Paley's 1785 book *The Principles of Moral and Political Philosophy*. In 1835, Mill published a review of Sedgwick's book in the *London Review*.	In1, IIn6, IIn9, App. A
"Taylor's Statesman," CW vol. XIX, pp. 617–47	In 1836, Henry Taylor, an English dramatist and poet, published *The Statesman*, a collection of essays on politics. In April 1837, Mill and George Grote published a review of Taylor's book in the *London and Westminster Review*.	App. A
"Carlyle's French Revolution," CW vol. XX, pp. 131–66	In 1837, Thomas Carlyle, the Scottish philosopher and historian mentioned above, published *The French Revolution: A History*. In July 1837, Mill published a review of Carlyle's book in the *London and Westminster Review*.	App. A

Work	Information	Location
"Bentham," CW vol. X, pp. 75–115	In 1838, on the occasion of the publication of Bentham's collected works, Mill published an essay on Bentham in the *London and Westminster Review*. In a later printing it bore the title *An Estimate of Bentham's Philosophy*, though it is generally known simply by the title "Bentham."	IIn1, IIn5, IIn11, App. C
A System of Logic, CW vols. VII–VIII	In 1843, Mill published *A System of Logic, Ratiocinative and Inductive, Being a Connected View of the Principles of Evidence and the Methods of Scientific Investigation*. Over the next three decades, he revised this work seven times. In this edition of *Utilitarianism*, the wording of each remark is that of the last edition of the *Logic* (the 1872 edition) but is identified by the year of the edition in which substantively the same material first appeared (subject only to minor revisions in subsequent editions). In each case, that year is either 1843 or 1851.	IIn4, IIn6, IVn3, App. A, App. C
"Whewell on Moral Philosophy," CW vol. X, pp. 165–201	In 1845, William Whewell, an English philosopher, published *Elements of Morality, including Polity*. In 1852, he published *Lectures on the History of Moral Philosophy in England*. Later in 1852, Mill published a review of Whewell's books in the *Westminster Review*.	In1, IIn1, IIn3, IIn7, IIn8, IIIn2, IVn2, App. A
Diary, CW vol. XXVII, pp. 639–68	Mill kept a diary for the first few months of 1854.	IIn2
Letter to Theodor Gomperz, CW vol. XIV, pp. 238–39	Theodor Gomperz was an Austrian scholar who translated many of Mill's works into German. This letter is dated August 19, 1854.	In1
On Liberty, CW vol. XVIII, pp. 213–310	In this book, published in February 1859, Mill presents an impassioned defense of individual liberty, with special emphasis on freedom of speech and freedom to live in the manner one chooses.	Vn3, App. B
Letter to William George Ward, CW vol. XV, pp. 646–50	William George Ward was an English theologian and philosopher. This letter is dated November 28, 1859.	IIIn4, Vn2
Utilitarianism, CW vol. X, pp. 203–59	*Utilitarianism* was first published as a series of articles in the October, November, and December 1861 issues of *Fraser's Magazine*.	Full text provided in this edition

Work	Information	Location
Letter to George Grote, CW vol. XV, pp. 761–64	George Grote was an English historian (and banker and member of Parliament) with whom Mill had a long association, including coauthorship of "Taylor's Statesman" in 1837 (see above). This letter is dated January 10, 1862.	IIn6, App. B
Letter to Samuel Bailey, CW vol. XV, pp. 824–25	Samuel Bailey was an English philosopher. This letter is dated January 21, 1863.	Vn2
"Austin on Jurisprudence," CW vol. XXI, pp. 165–205	John Austin was an English legal scholar. After his death in 1859, his wife, Sarah Austin, endeavored to have some of his works republished, and one result was an 1863 volume called *Lectures on Jurisprudence*. Mill reviewed that work in October 1863 in the *Edinburgh Review*.	Vn2
An Examination of Sir William Hamilton's Philosophy, CW vol. IX	William Hamilton was a Scottish philosopher. Mill's book about his thought was published in April 1865.	Vn2
Auguste Comte and Positivism, CW vol. X, pp. 261–368	Auguste Comte was a French philosopher. In April and July 1865, Mill published two articles on Comte's work in the *Westminster Review*.	App. B
Letter to Henry S. Brandreth, CW vol. XVI, p. 1234	Henry S. Brandreth was a barrister who asked Mill about some aspects of utilitarianism. Mill's reply is dated February 9, 1867.	App. B
Letter to E. W. Young, CW vol. XVI, pp. 1327–28	E. W. Young asked Mill about some of his claims occurring near the end of *Utilitarianism*. Mill's reply is dated November 10, 1867.	Vn4, App. A
Letter to Henry Sidgwick, CW vol. XXXII, p. 185	Henry Sidgwick was an English philosopher. Like Mill's *Utilitarianism*, Sidgwick's *The Methods of Ethics* (the first edition of which was published in 1874) is widely regarded as one of the seminal texts in the history of utilitarian thought. This letter is dated November 26, 1867.	IIn1
Letter to Henry Jones, CW vol. XVI, pp. 1413–14	Henry Jones was a teacher in England who asked Mill about material in Chapter IV of *Utilitarianism*. This letter is dated June 13, 1868.	IVn1

Work	Information	Location
James Mill's Analysis of the Phenomena of the Human Mind, CW vol. XXXI, pp. 93–253	James Mill, John Stuart Mill's father, had published *Analysis of the Phenomena of the Human Mind* in 1829. In March 1869, a new edition was published, with commentary by John Stuart Mill and other scholars. Mill's preface and notes are collected separately.	IIn5, IVn2, Vn2
The Subjection of Women, CW vol. XXI, pp. 259–340	In this book, published in May 1869, Mill argues for the equality of women vis-à-vis men, with penetrating critiques of existing practices in realms such as marriage, politics, and the workplace.	App. A
"Thornton on Labour and Its Claims," CW vol. V, pp. 631–68	In 1869, William Thomas Thornton, an English economist who was also Mill's friend and coworker at the East India Company, published *On Labour, its Wrongful Claims and Rightful Dues, its Actual Present and Possible Future.* In May and June 1869, Mill published a review of Thornton's book in the *Fortnightly Review.*	App. A, App. B
"Berkeley's Life and Writings," CW vol. XI, pp. 449–71	George Berkeley was an Irish philosopher. This essay was published in the *Fortnightly Review* in 1871, on the occasion of the publication of Berkeley's collected works.	App. A
Letter to John Venn, CW vol. XVII, pp. 1881–82	John Venn was an English logician (after whom the Venn diagram is named). This letter is dated April 14, 1872.	IIn7
Autobiography, CW vol. I, pp. 1–290	Mill's *Autobiography* was published in November 1873, six months after his death.	In1, IIIn3

Mill wrote multiple letters to some of the correspondents mentioned in the table. Speaking precisely, then, some of the letters should be referred to using phrases such as "*one of* Mill's letters to John Venn." For simplicity, however, in this edition they will be referred to with phrases such as "Mill's letter to John Venn."

Introduction to *Utilitarianism*

My purpose in this section is to give you some background information that will help you understand *Utilitarianism*. If there is one line that sums up the main point of Mill's essay, it is this one: "actions are right in proportion as they tend to promote happiness, wrong as they tend to produce the reverse of happiness" (paragraph II.2). It is helpful to keep this in mind throughout. Beyond that, though, since the topics of the five chapters of *Utilitarianism* are rather distinct from each other, I will simply discuss the chapters one at a time. My aim is not to summarize the chapters but to mention some key ideas that can make your first reading of each chapter easier and more meaningful.

Chapter I: General Remarks

Mill begins *Utilitarianism* by situating it in relation to an important rival approach. Today, most first-time readers of Mill's essay are taught to contrast utilitarianism with another particular moral theory such as that of Immanuel Kant, but Mill takes a wider perspective. He does mention Kant's moral theory as a rival, but for Mill this contrast is an instance of a more fundamental contrast, between two ways of understanding how people can come to hold justified beliefs about morality. These two rival views, or "schools" (to use Mill's word), are the intuitive school and the inductive school. The intuitive school clashed with utilitarianism, while the inductive one was Mill's approach.

The distinctive tenet of the intuitive school, as Mill understood it, was that ordinary people have a particular innate mental faculty—a moral sense, a form of intuition—that enables them to distinguish between true (or sound or genuine) moral principles and false (or unsound or impostor) moral principles. For example, according to intuitionists, if people were considering whether women should be given the right to vote (which they did not have, in the England of Mill's time), each person should calmly ponder the question to see what his or her moral sense had to say. A well-functioning moral sense would provide a person with a sound judgment on that issue, just as directly as other senses distinguish red versus blue and sweet versus bitter.

Mill saw no reason to believe in the existence of a moral sense. This does not mean that he thought that moral knowledge was unattainable;

rather, he just thought that moral knowledge was to be arrived at in much the same way as a lot of other knowledge: through experiencing ordinary life, being observant and inquisitive about how existing practices and institutions work, and considering alternative policies and courses of action as carefully as circumstances permit. In short, moral knowledge is to be attained by way of the same sort of inductive reasoning that is used to attain scientific knowledge. Within this model, the issue of women's suffrage should be decided by thinking about why women have tradition-ally been excluded from voting, what consequences have resulted from this policy, what would probably happen if this policy were changed, and so on. A person's simple pronouncement that his moral sense told him that women should be denied the vote (or that they should be granted it) should be regarded as nothing more than an unsupported opinion.

Mill preferred the inductive approach for many reasons. First, it avoids making a dubious psychological assumption about a special mental fac-ulty; rather, it relies on the same sort of reasoning that works well in many other areas of thought. In addition, it handles cases of disagreement better: whereas intuitionists cannot provide much guidance for dealing with a brute clash of opinion, inductivists encourage further inquiry and discussion that might well resolve (or at least lessen) the disagreement. Finally, the inductive approach fosters progress in moral thinking. Mill was particularly persistent on this last point; he says in several places that when people think about ethics by appealing to nothing more than intuition, they tend to endorse existing practices and institutions without noticing how they can be improved.

Chapter II: What Utilitarianism Is

Chapter II is the most important chapter of *Utilitarianism*. Although it covers the topic suggested by its title, the vast majority of the chapter consists of Mill's statements of, and replies to, nearly a dozen different objections to utilitarianism. One might have expected that before dis-cussing objections, Mill would have provided one or more arguments in support of his view, but he delays that until the fourth chapter. More urgent, for Mill, is addressing objections that he worries might already be in the minds of his readers, and might (until being addressed) make them less receptive to other things he has to say about utilitarianism. For the most part, Mill's strategy for responding to these objections is to say that while they are motivated by valid concerns about moral theorizing, they pertain to errors and failings that utilitarianism is not actually guilty of. In other words, once utilitarianism is properly understood, many of these objections are seen to be inapplicable. In this way, the title of the chapter is more appropriate than might initially be apparent: saying what utilitarianism is (partly by saying what it is *not*) disposes of many objections.

Chapter II raises many issues, but two have attracted much more attention than the rest. The first of these is Mill's higher pleasures doctrine (paragraphs II.3–II.9). This doctrine is not found in the work of earlier utilitarians; it is a new doctrine that Mill introduces here in order to address a standard objection to utilitarianism. This objection is that by conceiving of what is good for people entirely in terms of pleasure and the absence of pain, utilitarianism emphasizes activities such as eating, drinking, and sex, and overlooks the value of endeavors such as mental cultivation, long-term relationships, and living with integrity. To address this objection, Mill acknowledges the value of such mental pursuits but claims that they *are* pleasures, no less than bodily pleasures are. He also holds that these mental pursuits can even be more pleasurable, purely in terms of quantity of pleasure, than bodily pleasures are. Moreover—and here is Mill's new claim—they are of a different and higher *quality* than bodily pleasures, and this matters alongside quantity. This is Mill's higher pleasures doctrine. (The word "higher" refers to the higher *quality* Mill believes some pleasures have.) This doctrine means that a smaller quantity of a higher pleasure can be more valuable, and add more to a person's happiness, than a larger quantity of a lower pleasure. In this view of pleasures, a theory based on pleasure is perfectly capable of recommending an elevated and dignified kind of life.

The breadth of Mill's conception of pleasures—encompassing mental as well as bodily pleasures—is generally uncontroversial. But his higher pleasures doctrine has attracted consternation and criticism, because of its attempt to include qualitative as well as quantitative comparisons of pleasures. To many readers, it has seemed as if Mill's doctrine must be vulnerable to one of two possible objections. One objection is that Mill's qualitative differences are ultimately the same as plain old quantitative differences. For example, suppose a person teaches an excellent philosophy class and then eats a bowl of ice cream. One might say (following Mill) that the teaching pleasure is of a higher *quality* than the eating pleasure, but according to the objection we are now considering, this reference to quality serves no purpose: it amounts to nothing more than saying that the teaching is simply *more* pleasurable, all things considered, than the eating. In other words, we could just compare them quantitatively. The other objection allows that qualitative differences might amount to something other than quantitative differences, but holds that Mill must be relying on some additional criterion, aside from pleasure, in order to distinguish some pleasures as "higher quality." These possible objections are both damaging to Mill because if the first objection is true, then there is really nothing new about Mill's discussion of pleasures, except for some inflated and ultimately superfluous terminology; and if the second objection is true, then Mill is relying on some additional ideas that he leaves unspecified and unexplained.

The other major issue of Chapter II is arguably the most extensively debated interpretive question about *Utilitarianism* as a whole. This is the question of which (if either) of two major forms of utilitarianism—"act utilitarianism" and "rule utilitarianism"—Mill should be understood as an early proponent of. Before explaining these two views, let me mention that Mill does not explicitly endorse either one. The terms themselves were not coined for another hundred years, and it is not even clear which side of the distinction Mill belongs on.

To comprehend these two views, consider a situation in which a person is deciding whether to cheat on her taxes. Suppose the person intends to use the extra money for a good purpose, such as dental care for impoverished children, and suppose that act would, in fact, produce more happiness than filing her taxes honestly would. In forming a moral judgment, one approach you might take is to say that since cheating would produce more happiness in this situation, it is the right thing to do (again, in this situation). This is the approach of act utilitarianism, which is the simplest and most straightforward form of utilitarianism. It holds that an act is right if and only if it results in at least as much overall happiness as any act the agent could have performed. Each situation is to be examined individually, and the right act in any situation is the act that produces the most happiness.

Another approach you might take to the tax situation is to imagine what society would be like if, in general, people cheated on their taxes whenever they believed that doing so would produce more happiness. The results would be awful, due to the breakdown of basic government services (or astronomical enforcement costs for tax collection). On this basis, you might conclude that cheating is wrong, and that there ought to be a rule against it, even in the specific case we are considering. This approach captures the gist of rule utilitarianism. Rather than evaluating individual acts directly in terms of their effects on happiness, rule utilitarianism evaluates possible moral rules in terms of their effects on happiness, and then evaluates acts in terms of their conformity to the most happiness-promoting rules. Specifically, rule utilitarianism holds that an act is right if and only if it would be permitted by a system of rules whose general acceptance would result in at least as much overall happiness as would the general acceptance of any system of rules. Most proponents of rule utilitarianism say that the system of rules that would produce the most happiness includes many of the rules of commonsense morality: tell the truth, keep your promises, respect other people's rights, pay your taxes, and so on (perhaps with refinements in some cases).

Act and rule utilitarianism often agree, since the rules that produce the most happiness often permit the acts that produce the most happiness. But sometimes, as in the tax situation just discussed, they disagree. The conflict between them is largely about the role of rules in morality: whether they are integral to morality or just optional tools for decision making. Throughout *Utilitarianism* there are remarks that seem to support one of these conceptions of rules or the other, but the densest concentration of such remarks is found in the final seven paragraphs of Chapter II (paragraphs II.19–II.25).

Chapter III: Of the Ultimate Sanction of the Principle of Utility

This short chapter concerns how people can be motivated to comply with the requirements of utilitarian morality in everyday life. Mill puts the question in terms of the possible "sanctions" of utilitarianism—the influences that might, if directed appropriately, motivate people to comply with utilitarianism.

Mill's general strategy for vindicating utilitarianism along this dimension of evaluation is to say that whatever sanctions work in favor of other moral outlooks (whether a rival theory or just commonsense morality) can work equally well in favor of utilitarianism. First, he briefly discusses "external" sanctions. These include social pressure and (even when one does not feel pressure) the unselfish desire to please other people, and similar attitudes toward God—either fear of punishment from God or a devout desire to please God. He claims that these sanctions can motivate people to comply with utilitarianism just as much as any other moral outlook. Then, at much greater length (starting with paragraph III.4),

Mill discusses what he calls the "internal" sanction—the conscience. (This is the basis of the chapter's title.) Mill argues that this sanction can be strongly supportive of utilitarianism. He claims that people's consciences are shaped by influences such as parents, teachers, and peers, and that if these influences promoted utilitarian ways of thinking, then people's consciences would naturally develop in that direction. Mill is not claiming that accomplishing such a massive social transformation is within his power, only that the sanction of conscience *could* (if given the right kind of nurturing) support utilitarianism just as much as it could or does support any other moral outlook.

Chapter IV: Of What Sort of Proof the Principle of Utility Is Susceptible

As mentioned above (in connection with Chapter II), the fourth chapter is where Mill argues in support of the truth of utilitarianism. In particular, he argues in support of utilitarianism's claim that overall happiness is the ultimate goal or purpose of morality. His argument is based on observable facts of human psychology (in line with his support, in Chapter I, of doing moral philosophy inductively): he claims that happiness is all that people actually ultimately desire and that therefore, happiness is all that is ultimately desirable, both on an individual level and on an aggregate, or overall, level.

Oddly, the most-discussed aspects of this chapter are two passages that many critics have taken to exhibit embarrassing logical fallacies. The first is the passage in which Mill claims that the best way to figure out what is worthy of being desired—what morality should be concerned with—is to see what people actually desire. For example, if one were trying to figure out whether happiness is morally good, or whether death is morally good, or whether marble statues are morally good, one should just find out what people think about those things. The way Mill puts this is that "the sole evidence it is possible to produce that anything is desirable, is that people do actually desire it" (paragraph IV.3). Taken in isolation, this claim might be debatable, but it would not be preposterous. But this claim is immediately preceded by the sentence "The only proof capable of being given that an object is visible, is that people actually see it" and a similar sentence about a sound being audible. Unfortunately, these sentences have caused many critics to think that Mill's sentence about what is desirable is fatally flawed.

What these critics say is that in Mill's argument, the word "desirable" refers to not only the concept *worthy of being desired* (mentioned above) but also the concept *capable of being desired* (suggested by the words "visible" and "audible"). These two concepts are importantly different: the first evaluates something approvingly, while the second merely notes that something might be approvingly evaluated by some people, without taking any stand on whether they would be correct in taking that approving attitude toward it. If the critics are right that both meanings are involved in Mill's argument, then the argument would fall apart—in a good argument, a crucial word cannot change meanings partway through. When that happens, the author is said to have "equivocated," or been indecisive and ambiguous, about the meaning of that word. Consequently, this problem is called the "fallacy of equivocation." Defenders of Mill point out that he was not only a moralist but also a logician—indeed, such an accomplished logician that it is probably a misinterpretation to think he would make such a silly blunder. In regard to this particular passage, defenders say Mill's argument does not depend on the word "desirable" referring to the concept *capable of being desired*, and that his references to visibility and audibility are meant merely as rough illustrations.

The other most discussed passage occurs later in the same paragraph, when Mill argues from the desirability of happiness on an individual level to the desirability of happiness on an overall level. He writes, "No reason can be given why the general happiness is desirable, except that each person [. . .] desires his own happiness. [. . .] [E]ach person's happiness is a good to that person, and the general happiness, therefore, a good to the aggregate of all persons." Some critics say that here, Mill is committing the "fallacy of composition," which occurs when some items have a particular characteristic and the author then infers that anything composed of those items must also have that same characteristic. (A standard example is the following: atoms are colorless; therefore, things composed of atoms are colorless.) Mill himself offered a clarification of this passage in a letter, excerpted in the first endnote provided for Chapter IV.

Those two controversial passages occur very near the beginning of the chapter. The rest of the chapter—which is more than four fifths of it—is concerned with potential counterexamples to Mill's claim that happiness is all that people ultimately desire. For example, an objector might say that some people also ultimately desire virtue, or money. Mill's strategy for dealing with such objections is not to deny the phenomena that the objections are based on (you cannot deny that people desire money, for example), but to attempt to describe those phenomena as consistent with his view, so that they do not end up being counterexamples. Consequently, the majority of Chapter IV is actually psychology: specifically, how we should understand what is going on when people are in states of desiring and related states such as willing, choosing, pursuing, and so on.

Chapter V: On the Connexion between Justice and Utility

In the final (and longest) chapter of *Utilitarianism*, Mill conducts an extensive investigation into the idea of justice and how utilitarianism relates to it. He acknowledges that justice is a cherished moral ideal and that many people perceive utilitarianism to be comparatively deficient. People think of justice as principled, uncompromising, and definitely not derived from or subordinate to calculations about increasing and decreasing happiness. Consequently, they react with suspicion to the idea that happiness is the sole basis of morality. Mill's response to this objection follows a strategy we have seen him use before (particularly in Chapters II and IV): instead of arguing against the opinion underlying the objection—in this case, the profound regard many people have for the idea of justice—he argues that it can be accommodated within his framework. Mill does this by saying that the central requirements of justice—rules for the security of people and their property—are essential devices for the promotion of happiness, and hence high-priority implications of utilitarianism. For example, everyone would agree that if a sheriff were to seize someone's home, sell it, and pocket the proceeds, such misconduct would violate a rule of justice. Mill would simply want to point out that such a rule would also clearly be required by utilitarianism, since such misconduct would clearly interfere with the promotion of happiness. Speaking more broadly, Mill's general strategy is to argue that utilitarianism can respectfully complement and provide a deeper foundation for a person's preexisting regard for justice, rather than clashing with it.

There is one other aspect of Chapter V that you will want to notice when you get to it. In paragraph V.14, Mill characterizes immoral actions not just in terms of failing to promote happiness, but also in terms of another concept: punishment. He writes, "We do not call anything wrong, unless we mean to imply that a person ought to be punished in some way or other for doing it." Although Mill says this as if it is a perfectly ordinary remark, it is actually a dramatic twist that seriously complicates Mill's view. After all, if the defining idea of utilitarianism is that "actions are right in proportion as they tend to promote happiness, wrong as they tend to produce the reverse of happiness" (from paragraph II.2, as quoted above), then punishment—specifically, which wrong actions should be punished, and how—would seem to be an entirely separate question. But Mill says punishment is an ingredient in the very idea of wrongness itself. Interpreters of *Utilitarianism* continue to debate the meaning of this crucial but perplexing paragraph.

Further Reading

There is a wealth of high-quality discussion of Mill's *Utilitarianism*. The following are relatively brief overviews:

- Roger Crisp, introductory material and notes in his edition of Mill's *Utilitarianism* (Oxford University Press, 1998).

- Wendy Donner, "Mill's utilitarianism," in *The Cambridge Companion to Mill* (Cambridge University Press, 1998), pp. 252–92. This chapter is available online at http://dx.doi.org/10.1017/CCOL0521419875.008. Access is restricted but some universities have subscriptions enabling free access on campus.

- Christopher Macleod, "John Stuart Mill" entry in the *Stanford Encyclopedia of Philosophy*, sections 4.1–4.3 (on practical reason, happiness, and morality). Available online (and free) at http://plato. stanford.edu/entries/mill.

- John Skorupski, *Why Read Mill Today?* (Routledge, 2006), chapter 2: "The Good for Human Beings."

- Henry R. West, "Mill and utilitarianism in the mid-nineteenth century," in *The Cambridge Companion to Utilitarianism* (Cambridge University Press, 2014), pp. 61–80. This chapter is available online at http://dx.doi.org/10.1017/CCO9781139096737.004. Access is restricted but some universities have subscriptions enabling free access on campus.

- Fred Wilson, "John Stuart Mill" entry in the *Stanford Encyclopedia of Philosophy*, section 12: "Moral Philosophy: Utilitarianism." Available online (and free) at http://plato.stanford.edu/archives/spr2016/entries/mill. (In 2016 this entry was replaced by the "John Stuart Mill" entry written by Christopher Macleod, mentioned above.)

For longer resources, see the books listed in the Acknowledgments, and the following:

- David O. Brink, "Mill's Moral and Political Philosophy" entry in the *Stanford Encyclopedia of Philosophy*, section 2: "Mill's Utilitarianism." Available online (and free) at http://plato.stanford.edu/entries/mill-moral-political.

Part 2:

Utilitarianism *and Related Remarks*

Chapter I: General Remarks

There are few circumstances among those which make up the present   I.1
condition of human knowledge, more unlike what might have been
expected, or more significant of the backward state in which speculation on the most important subjects still lingers, than the little progress
which has been made in the decision of the controversy respecting
the criterion of right and wrong. From the dawn of philosophy, the
question concerning the *summum bonum*, or, what is the same thing,
concerning the foundation of morality, has been accounted the main
problem in speculative thought, has occupied the most gifted intellects, and divided them into sects and schools, carrying on a vigorous
warfare against one another. And after more than two thousand years
the same discussions continue, philosophers are still ranged under the
same contending banners, and neither thinkers nor mankind at large
seem nearer to being unanimous on the subject, than when the youth
Socrates listened to the old Protagoras, and asserted (if Plato's dia-
logue be grounded on a real conversation) the theory of utilitarianism
against the popular morality of the so-called sophist.

It is true that similar confusion and uncertainty, and in some cases   I.2
similar discordance, exist respecting the first principles of all the sciences, not excepting that which is deemed the most certain of them,
mathematics; without much impairing, generally indeed without
impairing at all, the trustworthiness of the conclusions of those sciences. An apparent anomaly, the explanation of which is, that the
detailed doctrines of a science are not usually deduced from, nor
depend for their evidence upon, what are called its first principles.
Were it not so, there would be no science more precarious, or whose
conclusions were more insufficiently made out, than algebra; which
derives none of its certainty from what are commonly taught to learn-
ers as its elements, since these, as laid down by some of its most emi-
nent teachers, are as full of fictions as English law, and of mysteries as
theology. The truths which are ultimately accepted as the first principles of a science, are really the last results of metaphysical analysis,

practised on the elementary notions with which the science is conversant; and their relation to the science is not that of foundations to an edifice, but of roots to a tree, which may perform their office equally well though they be never dug down to and exposed to [p. 206] light. But though in science the particular truths precede the general theory, the contrary might be expected to be the case with a practical art, such as morals or legislation. All action is for the sake of some end, and rules of action, it seems natural to suppose, must take their whole character and colour from the end to which they are subservient. When we engage in a pursuit, a clear and precise conception of what we are pursuing would seem to be the first thing we need, instead of the last we are to look forward to. A test of right and wrong must be the means, one would think, of ascertaining what is right or wrong, and not a consequence of having already ascertained it.

I.3   The difficulty is not avoided by having recourse to the popular theory of a natural faculty, a sense or instinct, informing us of right and wrong. For—besides that the existence of such a moral instinct is itself one of the matters in dispute—those believers in it who have any pretensions to philosophy, have been obliged to abandon the idea that it discerns what is right or wrong in the particular case in hand, as our other senses discern the sight or sound actually present. Our moral faculty, according to all those of its interpreters who are entitled to the name of thinkers, supplies us only with the general principles of moral judgments; it is a branch of our reason, not of our sensitive faculty; and must be looked to for the abstract doctrines of morality, not for perception of it in the concrete. The intuitive, no less than what may be termed the inductive, school of ethics, insists on the necessity of general laws. They both agree that the morality of an individual action is not a question of direct perception, but of the application of a law to an individual case. They recognise also, to a great extent, the same moral laws; but differ as to their evidence, and the source from which they derive their authority. According to the one opinion, the principles of morals are evident *à priori*, requiring nothing to command assent, except that the meaning of the terms be understood. According to the other doctrine, right and wrong, as well as truth and falsehood, are questions of observation and experience. But both hold equally that morality must be deduced from principles; and the intuitive school affirm as strongly as the inductive, that there is a science of morals. Yet they seldom attempt to make out a list of the *à priori* principles which are to serve as the premises of the science; still more rarely do they make any effort to reduce those various principles to one first principle, or common ground of obligation. They either assume the ordinary precepts of morals as of *à priori* authority, or they lay down as the common groundwork of those maxims, some generality much less obviously authoritative than the maxims themselves, and which has never succeeded in gaining popular acceptance. Yet to support their pretensions there ought either to be some one fundamental principle or law, at the root of all morality, or if there be several, there should be a determinate order of precedence among them; [p. 207] and the one principle, or the rule for deciding between the various principles when they conflict, ought to be self-evident.[1]

To inquire how far the bad effects of this deficiency have been mitigated in practice, or to what extent the moral beliefs of mankind have been vitiated or made uncertain by the absence of any distinct recognition of an ultimate standard, would imply a complete survey and criticism of past and present ethical doctrine. It would, however, be easy to show that whatever steadiness or consistency these moral beliefs have attained, has been mainly due to the tacit influence of a standard not recognised. Although the non-existence of an acknowledged first principle has made ethics not so much a guide as a consecration of men's actual sentiments, still, as men's sentiments, both of favour and of aversion, are greatly influenced by what they suppose to be the effects of things upon their happiness, the principle of utility, or as Bentham latterly called it, the greatest happiness principle, has had a large share in forming the moral doctrines even of those who most scornfully reject its authority. Nor is there any school of thought which refuses to admit that the influence of actions on happiness is a most material and even predominant consideration in many of the details of morals, however unwilling to acknowledge it as the fundamental principle of morality, and the source of moral obligation. I might go much further, and say that to all those *à priori* moralists who deem it necessary to argue at all, utilitarian arguments are indispensable. It is not my present purpose to criticize these thinkers; but I cannot help referring, for illustration, to a systematic treatise by one of the most illustrious of them, the *Metaphysics of Ethics*, by Kant. This remarkable man, whose system of thought will long remain one of the landmarks in the history of philosophical speculation, does, in the treatise in question, lay down an universal first principle as the origin

I.4

and ground of moral obligation; it is this:—"So act, that the rule on which thou actest would admit of being adopted as a law by all rational beings." But when he begins to deduce from this precept any of the actual duties of morality, he fails, almost grotesquely, to show that there would be any contradiction, any logical (not to say physical) impossibility, in the adoption by all rational beings of the most outrageously immoral rules of conduct. All he shows is that the *consequences* of their universal adoption would be such as no one would choose to incur.

I.5   On the present occasion, I shall, without further discussion of the other theories, attempt to contribute something towards the understanding and appreciation of the Utilitarian or Happiness theory, and towards such proof as it is susceptible of. It is evident that this cannot be proof in the ordinary and popular meaning of the term. Questions of ultimate ends are not amenable to direct proof. Whatever can be proved to be good, must be so by being [p. 208] shown to be a means to something admitted to be good without proof. The medical art is proved to be good, by its conducing to health; but how is it possible to prove that health is good? The art of music is good, for the reason, among others, that it produces pleasure; but what proof is it possible to give that pleasure is good? If, then, it is asserted that there is a comprehensive formula, including all things which are in themselves good, and that what ever else is good, is not so as an end, but as a mean, the formula may be accepted or rejected, but is not a subject of what is commonly understood by proof. We are not, however, to infer that its acceptance or rejection must depend on blind impulse, or arbitrary choice. There is a larger meaning of the word proof, in which this question is as amenable to it as any other of the disputed questions of philosophy. The subject is within the cognizance of the rational faculty; and neither does that faculty deal with it solely in the way of intuition. Considerations may be presented capable of determining the intellect either to give or withhold its assent to the doctrine; and this is equivalent to proof.

I.6   We shall examine presently of what nature are these considerations; in what manner they apply to the case, and what rational grounds, therefore, can be given for accepting or rejecting the utilitarian formula. But it is a preliminary condition of rational acceptance or rejection, that the formula should be correctly understood. I believe that the very imperfect notion ordinarily formed of its meaning, is the chief obstacle which impedes its reception; and that could it be cleared, even from only the grosser misconceptions, the question would be greatly simplified, and a large proportion of its difficulties removed. Before, therefore, I attempt to enter into the philosophical grounds which can be given for assenting to the utilitarian standard, I shall offer some illustrations of the doctrine itself; with the view of showing more clearly what it is, distinguishing it from what it is not, and disposing of such of the practical objections to it as either originate in, or are closely connected with, mistaken interpretations of its meaning. Having thus prepared the ground, I shall afterwards endeavour to throw such light as I can upon the question, considered as one of philosophical theory.

Chapter I Endnotes

1. In paragraph I.3, Mill contrasts his inductive approach with the intuitionists' view that people have an innate moral faculty. The following remarks elaborate on this topic:

   a. From "Sedgwick's Discourse" (1835, CW vol. X, pp. 50–51):

   It is a fact in human nature, that we have moral judgments and moral feelings. We judge certain actions and dispositions to be right, others wrong: this we call approving and disapproving them. We have also feelings of pleasure in the contemplation of the former class of actions and dispositions—feelings of dislike and aversion to the latter; which feelings, as everybody must be [p. 51] conscious, do not exactly resemble any other of our feelings of pain or pleasure.

   Such are the phenomena. Concerning their reality there is no dispute. But there are two theories respecting the origin of these phenomena, which have divided philosophers from the earliest ages of philosophy. One is, that the distinction between right and wrong is an ultimate and inexplicable fact; that we perceive this distinction, as we perceive the distinction of colours, by a peculiar faculty; and that the pleasures and pains, the desires and aversions, consequent upon this perception, are all ultimate facts in our nature; as much so as the pleasures and pains, or the desires and aversions, of which sweet or bitter tastes, pleasing or grating sounds, are the object. This is called the theory of the moral sense—or of moral instincts—or of eternal and immutable morality—or of intuitive principles of morality—or by many other names; to the differences between which, those who adopt the theory often attach great importance, but which, for our present purpose, may all be considered as equivalent.

The other theory is, that the ideas of right and wrong, and the feelings which attach themselves to those ideas, are not ultimate facts, but may be explained and accounted for; are not the result of any peculiar law of our nature, but of the same laws on which all our other complex ideas and feelings depend: that the distinction between moral and immoral acts is not a peculiar and inscrutable property in the acts themselves, which we perceive by a sense, as we perceive colours by our sense of sight; but flows from the ordinary properties of those actions, for the recognition of which we need no other faculty than our intellects and our bodily senses. And the particular property in actions, which constitutes them moral or immoral, in the opinion of those who hold this theory (all of them, at least, who need here be noticed), is the influence of those actions, and of the dispositions from which they emanate, upon human happiness.

This theory is sometimes called the theory of Utility [. . .].

b. From "Sedgwick's Discourse" (1835, CW vol. X, pp. 73–74):

Not to mention the importance, to those who are entrusted with the education of the moral sentiments, of just views respecting their origin and nature; we may remark that, upon the truth or falseness of the doctrine of a moral sense, it depends whether morality is a fixed or a progressive body of doctrine. If it be true that man [p. 74] has a sense given him to determine what is right and wrong, it follows that his moral judgments and feelings cannot be susceptible of any improvement; such as they are they ought to remain. The question, what mankind in general ought to think and feel on the subject of their duty, must be determined by observing what, when no interest or passion can be seen to bias them, they think and feel already. According to the theory of utility, on the contrary, the question, what is our duty, is as open to discussion as any other question. Moral doctrines are no more to be received without evidence, nor to be sifted less carefully, than any other doctrines. An appeal lies, as on all other subjects, from a received opinion, however generally entertained, to the decisions of cultivated reason. The weakness of human intellect, and all the other infirmities of our nature, are considered to interfere as much with the rectitude of our judgments on morality, as on any other of our concerns; and changes as great are anticipated in our opinions on that subject, as on every other, both from the progress of intelligence, from more authentic and enlarged experience, and from alterations in the condition of the human race, requiring altered rules of conduct.

c.   From "Whewell on Moral Philosophy" (1852, CW vol. X, p. 179):

The contest between the morality which appeals to an external standard, and that which grounds itself on internal conviction, is the contest of progressive morality against stationary—of reason and argument against the deification of mere opinion and habit. The doctrine that the existing order of things is the natural order, and that, being natural, all innovation upon it is criminal, is as vicious in morals, as it is now at last admitted to be in physics, and in society and government.

d.   From Mill's letter to Theodor Gomperz (1854, CW vol. XIV, p. 239):

[. . .] the theory of innate principles, so unfortunately patronized by the philosophers of your country, & which through their influence has become the prevailing philosophy throughout Europe. I consider that school of philosophy as the greatest speculative hindrance to the regeneration so urgently required, of man and society; which can never be effected under the influence of a philosophy which makes opinions their own proof, and feelings their own justification.

e.   From *Autobiography* (1873, CW vol. I, p. 269):

   Now, the difference between these two schools of philosophy, that of Intuition, and that of Experience and Association,
is not a mere matter of abstract speculation; it is full of practical consequences, and lies at the foundation of all the greatest
differences of practical opinion in an age of progress.

Chapter II: What Utilitarianism Is

A passing remark is all that needs be given to the ignorant blunder of supposing that those who stand up for utility as the test of right and wrong, use the term in that restricted and merely colloquial sense in which utility is opposed to pleasure. An apology is due to the philosophical opponents of utilitarianism, for even the momentary appearance of confounding them with any one capable of so absurd a misconception; which is the more extraordinary, inasmuch as the contrary accusation, of referring everything to pleasure, and that too in its grossest form, is another of the common charges against utilitarianism: and, as has been pointedly remarked by an able writer, the same sort of persons, and often the very same persons, denounce the theory "as impracticably dry when the word utility precedes the word pleasure, and as too practicably voluptuous when the word pleasure precedes the word utility." Those who know anything about the matter are aware that every writer, from Epicurus to Bentham, who maintained the theory of utility, meant by it, not something to be contradistinguished from pleasure, but pleasure itself, together with exemption from pain; and instead of opposing the useful to the agreeable or the ornamental, have always declared that the useful means these, among other things. Yet the common herd, including the herd of writers, not only in newspapers and periodicals, but in books of weight and pretension, are perpetually falling into this shallow mistake. Having caught up the word utilitarian, while knowing nothing whatever about it but its sound, they habitually express by it the rejection, or the neglect, of pleasure in some of its forms; of beauty, of ornament, or of amusement. Nor is the term thus ignorantly misapplied solely in disparagement, but occasionally in compliment; as though it implied superiority to frivolity and the mere pleasures of the moment. And this perverted use is the only one in which the word is popularly known, and the one from which the new generation are acquiring their sole notion of its meaning. Those who introduced the word, but who had for many years discontinued it as a distinctive appellation, may well feel themselves called upon to resume it, if by doing so they can hope to contribute anything towards rescuing it from this utter degradation.*

[p. 210]

II.2   The creed which accepts as the foundation of morals, Utility, or the Greatest Happiness Principle, holds that actions are right in proportion as they tend to promote happiness, wrong as they tend to produce the reverse of happiness. By happiness is intended pleasure, and the absence of pain; by unhappiness, pain, and the privation of pleasure. To give a clear view of the moral standard set up by the theory, much more requires to be said; in particular, what things it includes in the ideas of pain and pleasure; and to what extent this is left an open question. But these supplementary explanations do not affect the theory of life on which this theory of morality is grounded—namely, that pleasure, and freedom from pain, are the only things desirable as ends; and that all desirable things (which are as numerous in the utilitarian as in any other scheme) are desirable either for the pleasure inherent in themselves, or as means to the promotion of pleasure and the prevention of pain.[1]

II.3   Now, such a theory of life excites in many minds, and among them in some of the most estimable in feeling and purpose, inveterate dislike. To suppose that life has (as they express it) no higher end than pleasure—no better and nobler object of desire and pursuit—they designate as utterly mean and grovelling; as a doctrine worthy only of swine, to whom the followers of Epicurus were, at a very early period, contemptuously likened; and modern holders of the doctrine are occasionally made the subject of equally polite comparisons by its German, French, and English assailants.

II.4   When thus attacked, the Epicureans have always answered, that it is not they, but their accusers, who represent human nature in a degrading light; since the accusation supposes human beings to be

---

*The author of this essay has reason for believing himself to be the first person [p. 210] who brought the word utilitarian into use. He did not invent it, but adopted it from a passing expression in Mr. Galt's *Annals of the Parish.* After using it as a designation for several years, he and others abandoned it from a growing dislike to anything resembling a badge or watchword of sectarian distinction. But as a name for one single opinion, not a set of opinions—to denote the recognition of utility as a standard, not any particular way of applying it—the term supplies a want in the language, and offers, in many cases, a convenient mode of avoiding tiresome circumlocution.

capable of no pleasures except those of which swine are capable. If this supposition were true, the charge could not be gainsaid, but would then be no longer an imputation; for if the sources of pleasure were precisely the same to human beings and to swine, the rule of life which is good enough for the one would be good enough for the other. The comparison of the Epicurean life to that of beasts is felt as degrading, precisely because a beast's pleasures do not satisfy a human being's conceptions of happiness. Human beings have faculties more elevated than the animal appetites, and when once made conscious of them, do not regard anything as happiness which does not include their gratifica- [p. 211] tion. I do not, indeed, consider the Epicureans to have been by any means faultless in drawing out their scheme of consequences from the utilitarian principle. To do this in any suffi-cient manner, many Stoic, as well as Christian elements require to be included. But there is no known Epicurean theory of life which does not assign to the pleasures of the intellect, of the feelings and imagi-nation, and of the moral sentiments, a much higher value as pleasures than to those of mere sensation. It must be admitted, however, that utilitarian writers in general have placed the superiority of mental over bodily pleasures chiefly in the greater permanency, safety, uncost-liness, &c., of the former—that is, in their circumstantial advantages rather than in their intrinsic nature. And on all these points utilitarians have fully proved their case; but they might have taken the other, and, as it may be called, higher ground, with entire consistency. It is quite compatible with the principle of utility to recognise the fact, that some *kinds* of pleasure are more desirable and more valuable than oth-ers. It would be absurd that while, in estimating all other things, qual-ity is considered as well as quantity, the estimation of pleasures should be supposed to depend on quantity alone.

If I am asked, what I mean by difference of quality in pleasures, II.5 or what makes one pleasure more valuable than another, merely as a pleasure, except its being greater in amount, there is but one pos-sible answer. Of two pleasures, if there be one to which all or almost all who have experience of both give a decided preference, irrespec-tive of any feeling of moral obligation to prefer it, that is the more desirable pleasure. If one of the two is, by those who are competently acquainted with both, placed so far above the other that they prefer it, even though knowing it to be attended with a greater amount of discontent, and would not resign it for any quantity of the other pleasure which their nature is capable of, we are justified in ascribing to the preferred enjoyment a superiority in quality, so far outweighing quantity as to render it, in comparison, of small account.

II.6   Now it is an unquestionable fact that those who are equally acquainted with, and equally capable of appreciating and enjoying, both, do give a most marked preference to the manner of existence which employs their higher faculties. Few human creatures would consent to be changed into any of the lower animals, for a promise of the fullest allowance of a beast's pleasures; no intelligent human being would consent to be a fool, no instructed person would be an ignoramus, no person of feeling and conscience would be selfish and base, even though they should be persuaded that the fool, the dunce, or the rascal is better satisfied with his lot than they are with theirs. They would not resign what they possess more than he, for the most complete satisfaction of all the desires which they have in common with him. If they ever fancy they would, it is only in cases of unhappiness so extreme, that to escape from it they would exchange their lot for almost any other, however undesirable [p. 212] in their own eyes. A being of higher faculties requires more to make him happy, is capable probably of more acute suffering, and is certainly accessible to it at more points, than one of an inferior type; but in spite of these liabilities, he can never really wish to sink into what he feels to be a lower grade of existence. We may give what explanation we please of this unwillingness; we may attribute it to pride, a name which is given indiscriminately to some of the most and to some of the least estimable feelings of which mankind are capable; we may refer it to the love of liberty and personal independence, an appeal to which was with the Stoics one of the most effective means for the inculcation of it; to the love of power, or to the love of excitement, both of which do really enter into and contribute to it: but its most appropriate appellation is a sense of dignity, which all human beings possess in one form or other, and in some, though by no means in exact, proportion to their higher faculties, and which is so essential a part of the happiness of those in whom it is strong, that nothing which conflicts with it could be, otherwise than momentarily, an object of desire to them. Whoever supposes that this preference takes place at a sacrifice of happiness— that the superior being, in anything like equal circumstances, is not happier than the inferior—confounds the two very different ideas, of happiness, and content. It is indisputable that the being whose capacities of enjoyment are low, has the greatest chance of having them fully satisfied; and a highly-endowed being will always feel that any happiness which he can look for, as the world is constituted, is imperfect. But he can learn to bear its imperfections, if they are at all bearable; and they will not make him envy the being who is indeed unconscious of the imperfections, but only because he feels not at all the good which those imperfections qualify. It is better to be a human being dissatisfied than a pig satisfied; better to be Socrates dissatisfied than a fool satisfied. And if the fool, or the pig, is of a different opinion, it is because they only know their own side of the question. The other party to the comparison knows both sides.[2]

It may be objected, that many who are capable of the higher plea-   II.7
sures, occasionally, under the influence of temptation, postpone them to the lower. But this is quite compatible with a full appreciation of the intrinsic superiority of the higher. Men often, from infirmity of character, make their election for the nearer good, though they know it to be the less valuable; and this no less when the choice is between two bodily pleasures, than when it is between bodily and mental. They pursue sensual indulgences to the injury of health, though perfectly aware that health is the greater good. It may be further objected, that many who begin with youthful enthusiasm for everything noble, as they advance in years sink into indolence and selfishness. But I do not believe that those who undergo this very common change, voluntarily [p. 213] choose the lower description of pleasures in preference to the higher. I believe that before they devote themselves exclusively to the one, they have already become incapable of the other. Capacity for the nobler feelings is in most natures a very tender plant, easily killed, not only by hostile influences, but by mere want of sustenance; and in the majority of young persons it speedily dies away if the occupations to which their position in life has devoted them, and the society into which it has thrown them, are not favourable to keeping that higher capacity in exercise. Men lose their high aspirations as they lose their intellectual tastes, because they have not time or opportunity for indulging them; and they addict themselves to inferior pleasures, not because they deliberately prefer them, but because they are either the only ones to which they have access, or the only ones which they are any longer capable of enjoying. It may be questioned whether any one who has remained equally susceptible to both classes of pleasures, ever knowingly and calmly

preferred the lower; though many, in all ages, have broken down in an ineffectual attempt to combine both.

II.8   From this verdict of the only competent judges, I apprehend there can be no appeal. On a question which is the best worth having of two pleasures, or which of two modes of existence is the most grateful to the feelings, apart from its moral attributes and from its consequences, the judgment of those who are qualified by knowledge of both, or, if they differ, that of the majority among them, must be admitted as final. And there needs be the less hesitation to accept this judgment respecting the quality of pleasures, since there is no other tribunal to be referred to even on the question of quantity. What means are there of determining which is the acutest of two pains, or the intensest of two pleasurable sensations, except the general suffrage of those who are familiar with both? Neither pains nor pleasures are homogeneous, and pain is always heterogeneous with pleasure. What is there to decide whether a particular pleasure is worth purchasing at the cost of a particular pain, except the feelings and judgment of the experienced? When, therefore, those feelings and judgment declare the pleasures derived from the higher faculties to be preferable *in kind*, apart from the question of intensity, to those of which the animal nature, disjoined from the higher faculties, is susceptible, they are entitled on this subject to the same regard.

II.9   I have dwelt on this point, as being a necessary part of a perfectly just conception of Utility or Happiness, considered as the directive rule of human conduct. But it is by no means an indispensable condition to the acceptance of the utilitarian standard; for that standard is not the agent's own greatest happiness, but the greatest amount of happiness altogether; and if it may possibly be doubted whether a noble character is always the happier for its nobleness, there can be no doubt that it makes other people happier, and that the world in general is immensely a gainer by it. Utilitarianism, therefore, [p. 214] could only attain its end by the general cultivation of nobleness of character, even if each individual were only benefited by the nobleness of others, and his own, so far as happiness is concerned, were a sheer deduction from the benefit. But the bare enunciation of such an absurdity as this last, renders refutation superfluous.

II.10   According to the Greatest Happiness Principle, as above explained, the ultimate end, with reference to and for the sake of which all other things are desirable (whether we are considering our own good or that of other people), is an existence exempt as far as possible from pain, and as rich as possible in enjoyments, both in point of quantity and quality; the test of quality, and the rule for measuring it against quantity, being the preference felt by those who, in their opportunities of experience, to which must be added their habits of self-consciousness and self-observation, are best furnished with the means of comparison. This, being, according to the utilitarian opinion, the end of human action, is necessarily also the standard of morality; which may accordingly be defined, the rules and precepts for human conduct, by the observance of which an existence such as has been described might be, to the greatest extent possible, secured to all mankind; and not to them only, but, so far as the nature of things admits, to the whole sentient creation.[3]

Against this doctrine, however, arises another class of objectors, II.11 who say that happiness, in any form, cannot be the rational purpose of human life and action; because, in the first place, it is unattainable: and they contemptuously ask, What right hast thou to be happy? a question which Mr. Carlyle clenches by the addition, What right, a short time ago, hadst thou even *to be*? Next, they say, that men can do *without* happiness; that all noble human beings have felt this, and could not have become noble but by learning the lesson of Entsagen, or renunciation; which lesson, thoroughly learnt and submitted to, they affirm to be the beginning and necessary condition of all virtue.

The first of these objections would go to the root of the mat- II.12 ter were it well founded; for if no happiness is to be had at all by human beings, the attainment of it cannot be the end of morality, or of any rational conduct. Though, even in that case, something might still be said for the utilitarian theory; since utility includes not solely the pursuit of happiness, but the prevention or mitigation of unhappiness; and if the former aim be chimerical, there will be all the greater scope and more imperative need for the latter, so long at least as mankind think fit to live, and do not take refuge in the simultaneous act of suicide recommended under certain conditions by Novalis. When, how- [p. 215] ever, it is thus positively asserted to be impossible that human life should be happy, the assertion, if not something like a verbal quibble, is at least an exaggeration. If by happiness be meant a continuity of highly pleasurable excitement, it is evident enough that this is impossible. A state of exalted pleasure lasts only moments, or in some cases, and with some intermissions, hours or days, and is the occasional brilliant flash of enjoyment, not its permanent and steady flame. Of this the philosophers who have taught that happiness is the end of life were as fully aware as those who taunt them. The happiness which they meant was not a life of rapture; but moments of such, in an existence made up of few and transitory pains, many and various pleasures, with a decided predominance of the active over the passive, and having as the foundation of the whole, not to expect more from life than it is capable of bestowing. A life thus composed, to those who have been fortunate enough to obtain it, has always appeared worthy of the name of happiness. And such an existence is even now the lot of many, during some considerable portion of their lives. The present wretched education, and wretched social arrangements, are the only real hindrance to its being attainable by almost all.

II.13   The objectors perhaps may doubt whether human beings, if taught to consider happiness as the end of life, would be satisfied with such a moderate share of it. But great numbers of mankind have been satisfied with much less. The main constituents of a satisfied life appear to be two, either of which by itself is often found sufficient for the purpose: tranquillity, and excitement. With much tranquillity, many find that they can be content with very little pleasure: with much excitement, many can reconcile themselves to a considerable quantity of pain. There is assuredly no inherent impossibility in enabling even the mass of mankind to unite both; since the two are so far from being incompatible that they are in natural alliance, the prolongation of either being a preparation for, and exciting a wish for, the other. It is only those in whom indolence amounts to a vice, that do not desire excitement after an interval of repose; it is only those in whom the need of excitement is a disease, that feel the tranquillity which follows excitement dull and insipid, instead of pleasurable in direct proportion to the excitement which preceded it. When people who are tolerably fortunate in their outward lot do not find in life sufficient enjoyment to make it valuable to them, the cause generally is, caring for nobody but themselves. To those who have neither public nor private affections, the excitements of life are much curtailed, and in any case dwindle in value as the time approaches when all selfish interests must be terminated by death: while those who leave after them objects of personal affection, and especially those who have also cultivated a fellow-feeling with the collective interests of mankind, retain as lively an interest in life on the eve of death as in the vigour of youth and health. Next to selfishness, the principal cause which makes life unsatisfactory, is want of mental cultivation. [p. 216] A cultivated mind—I do not mean that of a philosopher, but any mind to which the fountains of knowledge have been opened, and which has been taught, in any tolerable degree, to exercise its faculties—finds sources of inexhaustible interest in all that surrounds it; in the objects of nature, the achievements of art, the imaginations of poetry, the incidents of history, the ways of mankind past and present, and their prospects in the future. It is possible, indeed, to become indifferent to all this, and that too without having exhausted a thousandth part of it; but only when one has had from the beginning no moral or human interest in these things, and has sought in them only the gratification of curiosity.

Now there is absolutely no reason in the nature of things why an amount of mental culture sufficient to give an intelligent interest in these objects of contemplation, should not be the inheritance of every one born in a civilized country. As little is there an inherent necessity that any human being should be a selfish egotist, devoid of every feeling or care but those which centre in his own miserable individuality. Something far superior to this is sufficiently common even now, to give ample earnest of what the human species may be made. Genuine private affections, and a sincere interest in the public good, are possible, though in unequal degrees, to every rightly brought up human being. In a world in which there is so much to interest, so much to enjoy, and so much also to correct and improve, every one who has this moderate amount of moral and intellectual requisites is capable of an existence which may be called enviable; and unless such a person, through bad laws, or subjection to the will of others, is denied the liberty to use the sources of happiness within his reach, he will not fail to find this enviable existence, if he escape the positive evils of life, the great sources of physical and mental suffering—such as indigence, disease, and the unkindness, worthlessness, or premature loss of objects of affection. The main stress of the problem lies, therefore, in the contest with these calamities, from which it is a rare good fortune entirely to escape; which, as things now are, cannot be obviated, and often cannot be in any material degree mitigated. Yet no one whose opinion deserves a moment's consideration can doubt that most of the great positive evils of the world are in themselves removable, and will, if human affairs continue to improve, be in the end reduced within narrow limits. Poverty, in any sense implying suffering, may be completely

II.14

extinguished by the wisdom of society, combined with the good sense and providence of individuals. Even that most intractable of enemies, disease, may be indefinitely reduced in dimensions by good physical and moral education, and proper control of noxious influences; while the progress of science holds out a promise for the future of still more direct conquests over this detestable foe. And every advance in that direction relieves us from some, not only of the chances which cut short our own lives, but, what concerns us still more, which deprive [p. 217] us of those in whom our happiness is wrapt up. As for vicissitudes of fortune, and other disappointments connected with worldly circumstances, these are principally the effect either of gross imprudence, of ill-regulated desires, or of bad or imperfect social institutions. All the grand sources, in short, of human suffering are in a great degree, many of them almost entirely, conquerable by human care and effort; and though their removal is grievously slow—though a long succession of generations will perish in the breach before the conquest is completed, and this world becomes all that, if will and knowledge were not wanting, it might easily be made—yet every mind sufficiently intelligent and generous to bear a part, however small and unconspicuous, in the endeavour, will draw a noble enjoyment from the contest itself, which he would not for any bribe in the form of selfish indulgence consent to be without.

II.15   And this leads to the true estimation of what is said by the objectors concerning the possibility, and the obligation, of learning to do without happiness. Unquestionably it is possible to do without happiness; it is done involuntarily by nineteen-twentieths of mankind, even in those parts of our present world which are least deep in barbarism; and it often has to be done voluntarily by the hero or the martyr, for the sake of something which he prizes more than his individual happiness. But this something, what is it, unless the happiness of others, or some of the requisites of happiness? It is noble to be capable of resigning entirely one's own portion of happiness, or chances of it: but, after all, this self-sacrifice must be for some end; it is not its own end; and if we are told that its end is not happiness, but virtue, which is better than happiness, I ask, would the sacrifice be made if the hero or martyr did not believe that it would earn for others immunity from similar sacrifices? Would it be made, if he thought that his renunciation of happiness for himself would produce no fruit for any of his fellow creatures, but to make their lot like his, and place them also in the condition of persons who have renounced happiness? All honour to those who can abnegate for themselves the personal enjoyment of life, when by such renunciation they contribute worthily to increase the amount of happiness in the world; but he who does it, or professes to do it, for any other purpose, is no more deserving of admiration than the ascetic mounted on his pillar. He may be an inspiriting proof of what men *can* do, but assuredly not an example of what they *should*.

Though it is only in a very imperfect state of the world's arrange- II.16 ments that any one can best serve the happiness of others by the absolute sacrifice of his own, yet so long as the world is in that imperfect state, I fully acknowledge that the readiness to make such a sacrifice is the highest virtue which can be found in man. I will add, that in this condition of the world, paradoxical as the assertion may be, the conscious ability to do without happiness gives the best prospect of realizing such happiness as is attainable. For [p. 218] nothing except that consciousness can raise a person above the chances of life, by making him feel that, let fate and fortune do their worst, they have not power to subdue him: which, once felt, frees him from excess of anxiety concerning the evils of life, and enables him, like many a Stoic in the worst times of the Roman Empire, to cultivate in tranquillity the sources of satisfaction accessible to him, without concerning himself about the uncertainty of their duration, any more than about their inevitable end.

Meanwhile, let utilitarians never cease to claim the morality of self- II.17 devotion as a possession which belongs by as good a right to them, as either to the Stoic or to the Transcendentalist. The utilitarian morality does recognise in human beings the power of sacrificing their own greatest good for the good of others. It only refuses to admit that the sacrifice is itself a good. A sacrifice which does not increase, or tend to increase, the sum total of happiness, it considers as wasted. The only self-renunciation which it applauds, is devotion to the happiness, or to some of the means of happiness, of others; either of mankind collectively, or of individuals within the limits imposed by the collective interests of mankind.

I must again repeat, what the assailants of utilitarianism seldom have II.18 the justice to acknowledge, that the happiness which forms the utilitarian standard of what is right in conduct, is not the agent's own happiness, but that of all concerned. As between his own happiness and that of others, utilitarianism requires him to be as strictly impartial as a disinterested and benevolent spectator. In the golden rule of Jesus of Nazareth, we read the complete spirit of the ethics of utility. To do as one would be done by, and to love one's neighbour as oneself, constitute the ideal perfection of utilitarian morality. As the means of making the nearest approach to this ideal, utility would enjoin, first, that laws and social arrangements should place the happiness, or (as speaking practically it may be called) the interest, of every individual, as nearly as possible in harmony with the interest of the whole; and secondly, that education and opinion, which have so vast a power over human character, should so use that power as to establish in the mind of every individual an indissoluble association between his own happiness and the good of the whole; especially between his own happiness and the practice of such modes of conduct, negative and positive, as regard for the universal happiness prescribes: so that not only he may be unable to conceive the possibility of happiness to himself, consistently with conduct opposed to the general good, but also that a direct impulse to promote the general good may be in every individual one of the habitual motives of action, and the sentiments connected therewith may fill a large and prominent place in every human being's sentient existence. If the impugners of the utilitarian morality [p. 219] represented it to their own minds in this its true character, I know not what recommendation possessed by any other morality they could possibly affirm to be wanting to it: what more beautiful or more exalted developments of human nature any other ethical system can be supposed to foster, or what springs of action, not accessible to the utilitarian, such systems rely on for giving effect to their mandates.

II.19   The objectors to utilitarianism cannot always be charged with representing it in a discreditable light. On the contrary, those among them who entertain anything like a just idea of its disinterested character, sometimes find fault with its standard as being too high for humanity. They say it is exacting too much to require that people shall always act from the inducement of promoting the general interests of society. But this is to mistake the very meaning of a standard of morals, and to confound the rule of action with the motive of it. It is the business of ethics to tell us what are our duties, or by what test we may know them; but no system of ethics requires that the sole motive of all we do shall be a feeling of duty; on the contrary, ninety-nine hundredths of all our actions are done from other motives, and rightly so done, if the rule of duty does not condemn them. It is the more unjust to utilitarianism that this particular misapprehension should be made a ground of objection to it, inasmuch as utilitarian moralists have gone beyond almost all others in affirming that the motive has nothing to do with the morality of the action, though much with the worth of the agent. He who saves a fellow creature from drowning does what is morally right, whether his motive be duty, or the hope of being paid for his trouble: he who betrays the friend that trusts him, is guilty of a crime, even if his object be to serve another friend to whom he is under greater obligations.* But to speak only of actions [p. 220] done from the motive of duty, and in direct obedience to principle: it is a misapprehension of the utilitarian mode of thought, to conceive it as implying that people should fix their minds upon so wide a generality as the world, or society at large. The great majority of good actions are intended, not for the benefit of the world, but for that of individuals,

---

*An opponent, whose intellectual and moral fairness it is a pleasure to acknowledge (the Rev. J. Llewellyn Davies), has objected to this passage, saying, "Surely the rightness or wrongness of saving a man from drowning does depend very much upon the motive with which it is done. Suppose that a tyrant, when his enemy jumped into the sea to escape from him, saved him from drowning simply in order that he might inflict upon him more exquisite tortures, would it tend to clearness to speak of that rescue as 'a morally right action?' Or suppose again, according to one of the stock illustrations of ethical inquiries, that a man betrayed a trust received from a friend, because the discharge of it would fatally injure that friend himself or some one belonging to him, would utilitarianism compel one to call the betrayal 'a crime' as much as if it had been done from the meanest motive?"

I submit, that he who saves another from drowning in order to kill him by torture afterwards, does not differ only in motive from him who does the same thing from duty or benevolence; the act itself is different. The rescue of the man is, in the case supposed, only the necessary first step of an act far more atrocious than leaving him to drown would have been.[4] Had Mr. Davies said, "The [p. 220] rightness or wrongness of saving a man from drowning does depend very much"—not upon the motive, but—"upon the *intention*," no utilitarian would have differed from him. Mr. Davies, by an oversight too common not to be quite venial, has in this case confounded the very different ideas of Motive and Intention. There is no point which utilitarian thinkers (and Bentham pre-eminently) have taken more pains to illustrate than this. The morality of the action depends entirely upon the intention—that is, upon what the agent *wills to do*.[5] But the motive, that is, the feeling which makes him will so to do, when it makes no difference in the act, makes none in the morality: though it makes a great difference in our moral estimation of the agent, especially if it indicates a good or a bad habitual *disposition*—a bent of character from which useful, or from which hurtful actions are likely to arise.

of which the good of the world is made up; and the thoughts of the most virtuous man need not on these occasions travel beyond the particular persons concerned, except so far as is necessary to assure himself that in benefiting them he is not violating the rights—that is, the legitimate and authorized expectations—of any one else. The multiplication of happiness is, according to the utilitarian ethics, the object of virtue: the occasions on which any person (except one in a thousand) has it in his power to do this on an extended scale, in other words, to be a public benefactor, are but exceptional; and on these occasions alone is he called on to consider public utility; in every other case, private utility, the interest or happiness of some few persons, is all he has to attend to. Those alone the influence of whose actions extends to society in general, need concern themselves habitually about so large an object.[6] In the case of abstinences indeed—of things which people forbear to do, from moral considerations, though the consequences in the particular case might be beneficial—it would be unworthy of an intelligent agent not to be consciously aware that the action is of a class which, if practised generally, would be generally injurious, and that this is the ground of the obligation to abstain from it.[7] The amount of regard for the public interest implied in this recognition, is no greater than is demanded by every system of morals; for they all enjoin to abstain from whatever is manifestly pernicious to society.

II.20   The same considerations dispose of another reproach against the doctrine of utility, founded on a still grosser misconception of the purpose of a standard of morality, and of the very meaning of the words right and wrong. It is often affirmed that utilitarianism renders men cold and unsympathizing; that it chills their moral feelings towards individuals; that it makes them regard only the dry and hard consideration of the consequences of actions, [p. 221] not taking into their moral estimate the qualities from which those actions emanate. If the assertion means that they do not allow their judgment respecting the rightness or wrongness of an action to be influenced by their opinion of the qualities of the person who does it, this is a complaint not against utilitarianism, but against having any standard of morality at all; for certainly no known ethical standard decides an action to be good or bad because it is done by a good or a bad man, still less because done by an amiable, a brave, or a benevolent man, or the contrary. These considerations are relevant, not to the estimation of actions, but of persons; and there is nothing in the utilitarian theory inconsistent with the fact that there are other things which interest us in persons besides the rightness and wrongness of their actions. The Stoics, indeed, with the paradoxical misuse of language which was part of their system, and by which they strove to raise themselves above all concern about anything but virtue, were fond of saying that he who has that has everything; that he, and only he, is rich, is beautiful, is a king. But no claim of this description is made for the virtuous man by the utilitarian doctrine. Utilitarians are quite aware that there are other desirable possessions and qualities besides virtue, and are perfectly willing to allow to all of them their full worth. They are also aware that a right action does not necessarily indicate a virtuous character, and that actions which are blameable often proceed from qualities entitled to praise. When this is apparent in any particular case, it modifies their estimation, not certainly of the act, but of the agent. I grant that they are, notwithstanding, of opinion, that in the long run the best proof of a good character is good actions; and resolutely refuse to consider any mental disposition as good, of which the predominant tendency is to produce bad conduct. This makes them unpopular with many people; but it is an unpopularity which they must share with every one who regards the distinction between right and wrong in a serious light; and the reproach is not one which a conscientious utilitarian need be anxious to repel.

If no more be meant by the objection than that many utilitarians look on the morality of actions, as measured by the utilitarian standard, with too exclusive a regard, and do not lay sufficient stress upon the other beauties of character which go towards making a human being loveable or admirable, this may be admitted. Utilitarians who have cultivated their moral feelings, but not their sympathies nor their artistic perceptions, do fall into this mistake; and so do all other moralists under the same conditions. What can be said in excuse for other moralists is equally available for them, namely, that if there is to be any error, it is better that it should be on that side. As a matter of fact, we may affirm that among utilitarians as among adherents of other systems, there is every imaginable degree of rigidity and of laxity in the application of their standard: some are even puritanically rigorous, while [p. 222] others are as indulgent as can possibly be desired by sinner or by sentimentalist. But on the whole, a doctrine which brings prominently forward the interest that mankind have in the repression and prevention of conduct which violates the moral law, is likely to be

II.21

inferior to no other in turning the sanctions of opinion against such violations. It is true, the question, What does violate the moral law? is one on which those who recognise different standards of morality are likely now and then to differ. But difference of opinion on moral questions was not first introduced into the world by utilitarianism, while that doctrine does supply, if not always an easy, at all events a tangible and intelligible mode of deciding such differences.

II.22   It may not be superfluous to notice a few more of the common misapprehensions of utilitarian ethics, even those which are so obvious and gross that it might appear impossible for any person of candour and intelligence to fall into them: since persons, even of considerable mental endowments, often give themselves so little trouble to understand the bearings of any opinion against which they entertain a prejudice, and men are in general so little conscious of this voluntary ignorance as a defect, that the vulgarest misunderstandings of ethical doctrines are continually met with in the deliberate writings of persons of the greatest pretensions both to high principle and to philosophy. We not uncommonly hear the doctrine of utility inveighed against as a *godless* doctrine. If it be necessary to say anything at all against so mere an assumption, we may say that the question depends upon what idea we have formed of the moral character of the Deity. If it be a true belief that God desires, above all things, the happiness of his creatures, and that this was his purpose in their creation, utility is not only not a godless doctrine, but more profoundly religious than any other. If it be meant that utilitarianism does not recognise the revealed will of God as the supreme law of morals, I answer, that an utilitarian who believes in the perfect goodness and wisdom of God, necessarily believes that whatever God has thought fit to reveal on the subject of morals, must fulfil the requirements of utility in a supreme degree. But others besides utilitarians have been of opinion that the Christian revelation was intended, and is fitted, to inform the hearts and minds of mankind with a spirit which should enable them to find for themselves what is right, and incline them to do it when found, rather than to tell them, except in a very general way, what it is: and that we need a doctrine of ethics, carefully followed out, to *interpret* to us the will of God. Whether this opinion is correct or not, it is superfluous here to discuss; since whatever aid religion, either natural or revealed, can afford to ethical investigation, is as open to the utilitarian moralist as to

any other. He can use it as the testimony of God to the usefulness or
hurtfulness of any given course of action, [p. 223] by as good a right as
others can use it for the indication of a transcendental law, having no
connexion with usefulness or with happiness.

Again, Utility is often summarily stigmatized as an immoral doc-   II.23
trine by giving it the name of Expediency, and taking advantage of the
popular use of that term to contrast it with Principle. But the Expedient, in the sense in which it is opposed to the Right, generally means
that which is expedient for the particular interest of the agent himself;
as when a minister sacrifices the interest of his country to keep himself
in place. When it means anything better than this, it means that which
is expedient for some immediate object, some temporary purpose, but
which violates a rule whose observance is expedient in a much higher
degree. The Expedient, in this sense, instead of being the same thing
with the useful, is a branch of the hurtful. Thus, it would often be
expedient, for the purpose of getting over some momentary embarrassment, or attaining some object immediately useful to ourselves
or others, to tell a lie. But inasmuch as the cultivation in ourselves
of a sensitive feeling on the subject of veracity, is one of the most
useful, and the enfeeblement of that feeling one of the most hurtful,
things to which our conduct can be instrumental; and inasmuch as
any, even unintentional, deviation from truth, does that much towards
weakening the trustworthiness of human assertion, which is not only
the principal support of all present social well-being, but the insuffi-
ciency of which does more than any one thing that can be named to
keep back civilization, virtue, everything on which human happiness
on the largest scale depends; we feel that the violation, for a present
advantage, of a rule of such transcendant expediency, is not expedient,
and that he who, for the sake of a convenience to himself or to some
other individual, does what depends on him to deprive mankind of
the good, and inflict upon them the evil, involved in the greater or
less reliance which they can place in each other's word, acts the part of
one of their worst enemies. Yet that even this rule, sacred as it is, admits
of possible exceptions, is acknowledged by all moralists; the chief of
which is when the withholding of some fact (as of information from a
malefactor, or of bad news from a person dangerously ill) would pre-
serve some one (especially a person other than oneself) from great and
unmerited evil, and when the withholding can only be effected by
denial. But in order that the exception may not extend itself beyond

the need, and may have the least possible effect in weakening reliance on veracity, it ought to be recognised, and, if possible, its limits defined;[8] and if the principle of utility is good for anything, it must be good for weighing these conflicting utilities against one another, and marking out the region within which one or the other preponderates. [p. 224]

II.24   Again, defenders of utility often find themselves called upon to reply to such objections as this—that there is not time, previous to action, for calculating and weighing the effects of any line of conduct on the general happiness. This is exactly as if any one were to say that it is impossible to guide our conduct by Christianity, because there is not time, on every occasion on which anything has to be done, to read through the Old and New Testaments. The answer to the objection is, that there has been ample time, namely, the whole past duration of the human species. During all that time mankind have been learning by experience the tendencies of actions; on which experience all the prudence, as well as all the morality of life, is dependent. People talk as if the commencement of this course of experience had hitherto been put off, and as if, at the moment when some man feels tempted to meddle with the property or life of another, he had to begin considering for the first time whether murder and theft are injurious to human happiness. Even then I do not think that he would find the question very puzzling; but, at all events, the matter is now done to his hand. It is truly a whimsical supposition that if mankind were agreed in considering utility to be the test of morality, they would remain without any agreement as to what *is* useful, and would take no measures for having their notions on the subject taught to the young, and enforced by law and opinion. There is no difficulty in proving any ethical standard whatever to work ill, if we suppose universal idiocy to be conjoined with it; but on any hypothesis short of that, mankind must by this time have acquired positive beliefs as to the effects of some actions on their happiness; and the beliefs which have thus come down are the rules of morality for the multitude, and for the philosopher until he has succeeded in finding better. That philosophers might easily do this, even now, on many subjects; that the received code of ethics is by no means of divine right; and that mankind have still much to learn as to the effects of actions on the general happiness, I admit, or rather, earnestly maintain. The corollaries from the principle of utility, like the precepts of every practical art, admit of indefinite improvement, and, in a progressive state of the human mind, their improvement is perpetually going on. But to consider the rules of morality as improvable, is one thing; to pass over the intermediate generalizations entirely, and endeavour to test each individual action directly by the first principle, is another. It is a strange notion that the acknowledgment of a first principle is inconsistent with the admission of secondary ones. To inform a traveller respecting the place of his ultimate destination, is not to forbid the use of landmarks and direction-posts on the way. The proposition that happiness is the end and aim of morality, does not mean that no road ought to be laid down to that goal, or that persons going thither should not be advised to [p. 225] take one direction rather than another. Men really ought to leave off talking a kind of nonsense on this subject, which they would neither talk nor listen to on other matters of practical concernment. Nobody argues that the art of navigation is not founded on astronomy, because sailors cannot wait to calculate the Nautical Almanack. Being rational creatures, they go to sea with it ready calculated; and all rational creatures go out upon the sea of life with their minds made up on the common questions of right and wrong, as well as on many of the far more difficult questions of wise and foolish. And this, as long as foresight is a human quality, it is to be presumed they will continue to do.[9] Whatever we adopt as the fundamental principle of morality, we require subordinate principles to apply it by: the impossibility of doing without them, being common to all systems, can afford no argument against any one in particular: but gravely to argue as if no such secondary principles could be had, and as if mankind had remained till now, and always must remain, without drawing any general conclusions from the experience of human life, is as high a pitch, I think, as absurdity has ever reached in philosophical controversy.

The remainder of the stock arguments against utilitarianism mostly consist in laying to its charge the common infirmities of human nature, and the general difficulties which embarrass conscientious persons in shaping their course through life. We are told that an utilitarian will be apt to make his own particular case an exception to moral rules, and, when under temptation, will see an utility in the breach of a rule, greater than he will see in its observance. But is utility the only creed which is able to furnish us with excuses for evil doing, and means of cheating our own conscience? They are afforded in abundance by all doctrines which recognise as a fact in morals the

II.25

existence of conflicting considerations; which all doctrines do, that have been believed by sane persons. It is not the fault of any creed, but of the complicated nature of human affairs, that rules of conduct cannot be so framed as to require no exceptions, and that hardly any kind of action can safely be laid down as either always obligatory or always condemnable.[10] There is no ethical creed which does not temper the rigidity of its laws, by giving a certain latitude, under the moral responsibility of the agent, for accommodation to peculiarities of circumstances; and under every creed, at the opening thus made, self-deception and dishonest casuistry get in. There exists no moral system under which there do not arise unequivocal cases of conflicting obligation. These are the real difficulties, the knotty points both in the theory of ethics, and in the conscientious guidance of personal conduct. They are overcome practically with greater or with less success according to the intellect and virtue of the individual; but it can hardly be pretended that any one will be the less qualified for dealing with them, from possessing an ultimate standard to which conflicting rights and duties can be referred. [p. 226] If utility is the ultimate source of moral obligations, utility may be invoked to decide between them when their demands are incompatible. Though the application of the standard may be difficult, it is better than none at all: while in other systems, the moral laws all claiming independent authority, there is no common umpire entitled to interfere between them; their claims to precedence one over another rest on little better than sophistry, and unless determined, as they generally are, by the unacknowledged influence of considerations of utility, afford a free scope for the action of personal desires and partialities. We must remember that only in these cases of conflict between secondary principles is it requisite that first principles should be appealed to.[11] There is no case of moral obligation in which some secondary principle is not involved; and if only one, there can seldom be any real doubt which one it is, in the mind of any person by whom the principle itself is recognised.

Chapter II Endnotes

1. The first sentence of paragraph II.2 ("The creed [. . .] holds that actions are right in proportion as they tend to promote happiness,

wrong as they tend to produce the reverse of happiness") is probably the most frequently quoted sentence of *Utilitarianism*. Similar remarks occur in a number of Mill's other works.

a. From "Brodie's History of the British Empire" (1824, CW vol. VI, p. 4):

[. . .] the only true end of morality, the greatest happiness of the greatest number [. . .]

b. From "Remarks on Bentham's Philosophy" (1833, CW vol. X, p. 5):

The first principles of Mr. Bentham's philosophy are these;—that happiness, meaning by that term pleasure and exemption from pain, is the only thing desirable in itself; that all other things are desirable solely as means to that end: that the production, therefore, of the greatest possible happiness, is the only fit purpose of all human thought and action, and consequently of all morality and government [. . .].

c. From "Bentham" (1838, CW vol. X, p. 111):

That the morality of actions depends on the consequences which they tend to produce, is the doctrine of rational persons of all schools; that the good or evil of those consequences is measured solely by pleasure or pain, is all of the doctrine of the school of utility, which is peculiar to it.

d. From "Whewell on Moral Philosophy" (1852, CW vol. X, p. 172):

[. . .] the tendency of actions to promote happiness affords a test to which the feelings of morality should conform.

e. From Mill's letter to Henry Sidgwick (1867, CW vol. XXXII, p. 185):

[. . .] the effect which actions tend to produce on human happiness is what constitutes them right or wrong.

2. In writing paragraphs II.2–II.6, Mill might have drawn on this entry in his *Diary* (1854, CW vol. XXVII, p. 663):

> The only true or definite rule of conduct or standard of morality is the greatest happiness, but there is needed first a philosophical estimate of happiness. Quality as well as quantity of happiness is to be considered; less of a higher kind is preferable to more of a lower. The test of quality is the preference given by those who are acquainted with both. Socrates would rather choose to be Socrates dissatisfied than to be a pig satisfied. The pig probably would not, but then the pig knows only one side of the question: Socrates knows both.

3. In the last sentence of paragraph II.10, Mill distinguishes between "the end of human action" and "the standard of morality." Mill seems to be alluding to his doctrine of the Art of Life; for Mill's main remarks on that topic, see Appendix C.

   Also in the last sentence of paragraph II.10, Mill briefly refers to "the whole sentient creation." Mill had previously affirmed the moral status of nonhuman animals quite forcefully in "Whewell on Moral Philosophy" (1852, CW vol. X, p. 187):

> We are perfectly willing to stake the whole question on this one issue. Granted that any practice causes more pain to animals than it gives pleasure to man; is that practice moral or immoral? And if, exactly in proportion as human beings raise their heads out of the slough of selfishness, they do not with one voice answer "immoral," let the morality of the principle of utility be for ever condemned.

4. In the footnote to paragraph II.19, Mill claims that "sav[ing] another from drowning in order to kill him by torture afterwards" is a different act from a normal rescue. This claim seems to rest on his conception of an act as comprising both volition and effect, as stated in *A System of Logic* (1843, CW vol. VII, p. 55):

> [. . .] what is an action? Not one thing, but a series of two things: the state of mind called a volition, followed by an effect. The volition or intention to produce the effect, is one

thing; the effect produced in consequence of the intention, is another thing; the two together constitute the action.

5. Later in the footnote to paragraph II.19, Mill claims that an act's morality depends only on the intention with which it is performed (and not at all on its other component, its effects). This claim is also found in the following remarks:

a. From "Bentham" (1838, CW vol. X, p. 112):

The morality of an action depends on its foreseeable consequences [. . .].

b. From *James Mill's Analysis of the Phenomena of the Human Mind* (1869, CW vol. XXXI, p. 253):

[. . .] it is the intention, that is, the foresight of consequences, which constitutes the moral rightness or wrongness of the act.

6. In paragraph II.19, Mill claims that most people can usually concern themselves with the happiness of just "some few persons." This is a point Mill made in some other remarks:

a. From Mill's letter to Thomas Carlyle (1834, CW vol. XII, pp. 207–8):

Though I hold the good of the species (or rather of its several units) to be the *ultimate* end, (which is the alpha & omega of my utilitarianism) I believe with the fullest Belief that this end can in no other way be forwarded but by the means you speak of, namely by each taking for his exclusive aim the development of what is best in [p. 208] *himself*. I qualify or explain this doctrine no otherwise than as you yourself do, since you hold that every human creature has an appointed task to perform which task he is to know & find out for himself; this can only be by discovering in what manner such faculties as he possesses or can acquire may produce most good in the world: meaning by the world a larger or a smaller part of it as may happen.

b.   From "Sedgwick's Discourse" (1835, CW vol. X, p. 59):

[. . .] none but those who mingle in public transactions, or whose example is likely to have extensive influence, have any occasion to look beyond the particular persons concerned. Morality, for all other people, consists in doing good and refraining from harm, to themselves and to those who immediately surround them.

c.   From sections that Mill added to the third edition (and retained in all subsequent editions) of *A System of Logic* (1851, CW vol. VIII, p. 952):

I do not mean to assert that the promotion of happiness should be itself the end of all actions, or even of all rules of action. It is the justification, and ought to be the controller, of all ends, but is not itself the sole end. There are many virtuous actions, and even virtuous modes of action (though the cases are, I think, less frequent than is often supposed) by which happiness in the particular instance is sacrificed, more pain being produced than pleasure. But conduct of which this can be truly asserted, admits of justification only because it can be shown that on the whole more happiness will exist in the world, if feelings are cultivated which will make people, in certain cases, regardless of happiness.

d.   From Mill's letter to George Grote (1862, CW vol. XV, p. 762):

The general happiness, looked upon as composed of as many different units as there are persons, all equal in value except as far as the amount of the happiness itself differs, leads to all the practical doctrines which you lay down. First, it requires that each shall consider it as his special business to take care of himself: the general good requiring that that one individual should be left, in all ordinary circumstances, to his own care, and not taken care of for him, further than by not impeding his own efforts, nor allowing others to do so. The good of all can only be pursued with any success by each person's taking as his particular department the good of the only individual

whose requirements he can thoroughly know; with due pre-
cautions to prevent these different persons, each cultivating a
particular strip of the field, from hindering one another.

7. The penultimate sentence of paragraph II.19 refers to abstaining
from actions on the basis of what the consequences would be if
they were "practised generally." The relevance of considering the
general performance of an action (even if one does not believe
that to be likely) is elaborated in the following passages.

    a.   In "Whewell on Moral Philosophy," Mill considers
Whewell's objection (to utilitarianism) that the wrongness
of certain acts cannot be accounted for in terms of
their consequences, because in many cases those
consequences are too small to be reliably measured.
Whewell says, for example, that although utilitarians
typically account for the wrongness of lying by saying
that lies "shake the general fabric of mutual human
confidence," their effects are usually undetectably small.
Mill replies as follows (1852, CW vol. X, pp. 181–82):

If the effect of a "solitary act upon the whole scheme of human
action and habit" is small, the addition which the accompany-
ing pleasure makes to the general mass of human happiness is
small likewise. So small, in the great majority of cases, are both,
that we have no scales to weigh them against each other, taken
singly. We must look at them multiplied, and in large masses.
The portion of the tendencies of an action which belong to
it not individually, but as a violation of a general rule, are as
certain and as calculable as any other consequences; only they
must be examined not in the individual case, but in classes of
cases. Take, for example, the case of murder. There are many
persons to kill whom would be to remove men who are a
cause of no good to any human being, of cruel physical and
moral suffering to several, and whose whole influence tends
to increase the mass of unhappiness and vice. Were such a
man to be assassinated, the balance of traceable consequences
would be greatly in favour of the act. The counter-consider-
ation, on the principle of utility, is, that unless [p. 182] persons

were punished for killing, and taught not to kill; that if it were thought allowable for any one to put to death at pleasure any human being whom he believes that the world would be well rid of, nobody's life would be safe. [. . .]

[. . .]

If a hundred infringements would produce all the mischief implied in the abrogation of the rule, a hundredth part of that mischief must be debited to each one of the infringements, though we may not be able to trace it home individually. And this hundredth part will generally far outweigh any good expected to arise from the individual act.

b. Mill also addresses this topic in his letter to John Venn (1872, CW vol. XVII, p. 1881–82):

I agree with you that the right way of testing actions by their consequences, is to test them by the natural consequences of the particular action, and not by those which would follow if every one did the same. But, for the most part, the consideration of what would happen if every one did the same, is the only means we have of discovering the tendency of the act in the particular case. In your example from Austria, it is only by considering what would happen if everybody evaded his share of taxation, that we perceive the mischievous tendency of anybody's doing so. And that this mischievous tendency overbalances (unless in very extreme cases) the private good obtained by the breach of a moral rule, is obvious if we take into consideration the importance, to the general good, of the feeling of security, or certainty; which is impaired, not only by every known [p. 1882] actual violation of good rules, but by the belief that such violations ever occur.

8. In paragraph II.23, Mill writes that exceptions to rules should be explicitly recognized and carefully defined. He had made much the same point in "Whewell on Moral Philosophy" (1852, CW vol. X, p. 183):

[. . .] the existence of exceptions to moral rules is no stumbling-block peculiar to the principle of utility. The essential is, that the exception should be itself a general rule; so that, being of definite extent, and not leaving the expediencies to the partial judgment of the agent in the individual case, it may not shake the stability of the wider rule in the cases to which the reason of the exception does not extend.

9. In paragraph II.24, Mill mentions the development of knowledge of the tendencies of actions during "the whole past duration of the human species" and uses his metaphor of the Nautical Almanack. He had used similar language (but with the spelling "Almanac") in "Sedgwick's Discourse" (1835, CW vol. X, pp. 65–66):

> Every one directs himself in morality, as in all his conduct, not by his own unaided [p. 66] foresight, but by the accumulated wisdom of all former ages, embodied in traditional aphorisms. [. . .] There is little fear, truly, that the mass of mankind should insist upon "tracing the consequences of actions" by their own unaided lights [. . .].
>
> Mr. Sedgwick is master of the stock phrases of those who know nothing of the principle of utility but the name. To act upon rules of conduct, of which utility is recognised as the basis, he calls "waiting for the calculations of utility"—a thing, according to him, in itself immoral, since "to hesitate is to rebel." On the same principle, navigating by rule instead of by instinct might be called waiting for the calculations of astronomy. There seems no absolute necessity for putting off the calculations until the ship is in the middle of the South Sea. Because a sailor has not verified all the computations in the Nautical Almanac, does he therefore "hesitate" to use it?

10. In paragraph II.25, Mill writes that "rules of conduct cannot be so framed as to require no exceptions," and similar language appears two paragraphs earlier. For more of Mill's remarks on this topic, see Appendix A.

11. Near the end of paragraph II.25, Mill writes that "only in these cases of conflict between secondary principles is it requisite that first principles should be appealed to." Similar remarks occur in at least two earlier works.

a. From "Blakey's History of Moral Science" (1833, CW
    vol. X, p. 29):

[. . .] a clear conception of the ultimate foundation of morality, is essential to a systematic and scientific treatment of the
subject, and to the decision of some of its disputed practical problems. But the most momentous of the differences of
opinion on the details of morality, have quite another origin.
The real character of any man's ethical system depends not on
his first and fundamental principle, which is of necessity so
general as to be rarely susceptible of an immediate application
to practice; but upon the nature of those secondary and intermediate maxims, *vera illa et media axiomata*, in which, as Bacon
observes, real wisdom resides. The grand consideration is, not
what any person regards as the ultimate end of human conduct, but through what intermediate ends he holds that his
ultimate end is attainable, and should be pursued: and in these
there is a nearer agreement between some who differ, than
between some who agree, in their conception of the ultimate
end. When disputes arise as to any of the secondary maxims, they can be decided, it is true, only by an appeal to first
principles; but the necessity of this appeal may be avoided far
oftener than is commonly believed; it is surprising how few,
in comparison, of the disputed questions of practical morals,
require for their determination any premises but such as are
common to all philosophic sects.

b. From "Bentham" (1838, CW vol. X, pp. 110–11):

We think utility, or happiness, much too complex and indefinite an end to be sought except through the medium of
various secondary ends, concerning which there may be, and
often is, agreement among persons who differ in their ultimate standard; and about which there does in fact prevail a
much greater unanimity among thinking persons, than might
be supposed from their diametrical divergence on the great
questions of moral metaphysics. As mankind are much more
nearly of one nature, than of one opinion about their own
nature, they [p. 111] are more easily brought to agree in their

intermediate principles, *vera illa et media axiomata*, as Bacon says, than in their first principles [. . .]. Those who adopt utility as a standard can seldom apply it truly except through the secondary principles; those who reject it, generally do no more than erect those secondary principles into first principles. It is when two or more of the secondary principles conflict, that a direct appeal to some first principle becomes necessary; and then commences the practical importance of the utilitarian controversy; which is, in other respects, a question of arrangement and logical subordination rather than of practice; important principally in a purely scientific point of view, for the sake of the systematic unity and coherency of ethical philosophy.

Chapter III: Of the Ultimate Sanction of the Principle of Utility

III.1   The question is often asked, and properly so, in regard to any supposed moral standard—What is its sanction? what are the motives to obey it? or more specifically, what is the source of its obligation? whence does it derive its binding force? It is a necessary part of moral philosophy to provide the answer to this question; which, though frequently assuming the shape of an objection to the utilitarian morality, as if it had some special applicability to that above others, really arises in regard to all standards. It arises, in fact, whenever a person is called on to *adopt* a standard, or refer morality to any basis on which he has not been accustomed to rest it. For the customary morality, that which education and opinion have consecrated, is the only one which presents itself to the mind with the feeling of being *in itself* obligatory; and when a person is asked to believe that this morality *derives* its obligation from some general principle round which custom has not thrown the same halo, the assertion is to him a paradox; the supposed corollaries seem to have a more binding force than the original theorem; the superstructure seems to stand better without, than with, what is represented as its foundation. He says to himself, I feel that I am bound not to rob or murder, betray or deceive; but why am I bound to promote the general happiness? If my own happiness lies in something else, why may I not give that the preference?

III.2   If the view adopted by the utilitarian philosophy of the nature of the moral sense be correct, this difficulty will always present itself, until the influences which form moral character have taken the same hold of the principle which they have taken of some of the consequences—until, by the improvement of education, the feeling of unity with our fellow creatures shall be (what it cannot be doubted that Christ intended it to be) as deeply rooted in our character, and to our own consciousness as completely a part of our nature, as the horror of crime is in an ordinarily well-brought up young person. In the mean time, however, the difficulty has no peculiar application to the doctrine of utility, but is inherent in every attempt to analyse morality and reduce [p. 228] it to principles; which, unless the principle is already in men's minds invested with as much sacredness as any of its applications, always seems to divest them of a part of their sanctity.

The principle of utility either has, or there is no reason why it might not have, all the sanctions which belong to any other system of morals. Those sanctions are either external or internal. Of the external sanctions it is not necessary to speak at any length. They are, the hope of favour and the fear of displeasure from our fellow creatures or from the Ruler of the Universe, along with whatever we may have of sympathy or affection for them, or of love and awe of Him, inclining us to do his will independently of selfish consequences. There is evidently no reason why all these motives for observance should not attach themselves to the utilitarian morality, as completely and as powerfully as to any other. Indeed, those of them which refer to our fellow creatures are sure to do so, in proportion to the amount of general intelligence; for whether there be any other ground of moral obligation than the general happiness or not, men do desire happiness; and however imperfect may be their own practice, they desire and commend all conduct in others towards themselves, by which they think their happiness is promoted. With regard to the religious motive, if men believe, as most profess to do, in the goodness of God, those who think that conduciveness to the general happiness is the essence, or even only the criterion, of good, must necessarily believe that it is also that which God approves. The whole force therefore of external reward and punishment, whether physical or moral, and whether proceeding from God or from our fellow men, together with all that the capacities of human nature admit, of disinterested devotion to either, become available to enforce the utilitarian morality, in proportion as that morality is recognised; and the more powerfully, the more the appliances of education and general cultivation are bent to the purpose.   III.3

So far as to external sanctions. The internal sanction of duty, whatever our standard of duty may be, is one and the same—a feeling in our own mind; a pain, more or less intense, attendant on violation of duty, which in properly-cultivated moral natures rises, in the more serious cases, into shrinking from it as an impossibility. This feeling, when disinterested, and connecting itself with the pure idea of duty,   III.4

and not with some particular form of it, or with any of the merely accessory circumstances, is the essence of Conscience; though in that complex phenomenon as it actually exists, the simple fact is in general all encrusted over with collateral associations, derived from sympathy, from love, and still more from fear; from all the forms of religious feeling; from the recollections of childhood and of all our past life; from self-esteem, desire of the esteem of others, and occasionally even self-abasement. This extreme complication is, I apprehend, the origin of the sort of mystical character which, by a tendency of the human mind of which there are [p. 229] many other examples, is apt to be attributed to the idea of moral obligation, and which leads people to believe that the idea cannot possibly attach itself to any other objects than those which, by a supposed mysterious law, are found in our present experience to excite it. Its binding force, however, consists in the existence of a mass of feeling which must be broken through in order to do what violates our standard of right, and which, if we do nevertheless violate that standard, will probably have to be encountered afterwards in the form of remorse.[1] Whatever theory we have of the nature or origin of conscience, this is what essentially constitutes it.

III.5   The ultimate sanction, therefore, of all morality (external motives apart) being a subjective feeling in our own minds, I see nothing embarrassing to those whose standard is utility, in the question, what is the sanction of that particular standard? We may answer, the same as of all other moral standards—the conscientious feelings of mankind. Undoubtedly this sanction has no binding efficacy on those who do not possess the feelings it appeals to; but neither will these persons be more obedient to any other moral principle than to the utilitarian one. On them morality of any kind has no hold but through the external sanctions. Meanwhile the feelings exist, a fact in human nature, the reality of which, and the great power with which they are capable of acting on those in whom they have been duly cultivated, are proved by experience. No reason has ever been shown why they may not be cultivated to as great intensity in connexion with the utilitarian, as with any other rule of morals.[2]

III.6   There is, I am aware, a disposition to believe that a person who sees in moral obligation a transcendental fact, an objective reality belonging to the province of "Things in themselves," is likely to be more obedient to it than one who believes it to be entirely subjective, having its seat in human consciousness only. But whatever a person's opinion may be on this point of Ontology, the force he is really urged by is his own subjective feeling, and is exactly measured by its strength. No one's belief that Duty is an objective reality is stronger than the belief that God is so; yet the belief in God, apart from the expectation of actual reward and punishment, only operates on conduct through, and in proportion to, the subjective religious feeling. The sanction, so far as it is disinterested, is always in the mind itself; and the notion therefore of the transcendental moralists must be, that this sanction will not exist *in* the mind unless it is believed to have its root out of the mind; and that if a person is able to say to himself, This which is restraining me, and which is called my conscience, is only a feeling in my own mind, he may possibly draw the conclusion that when the feeling ceases the obligation ceases, and that if he find the feeling inconvenient, he may disregard it, and endeavour to get rid of it. But is this danger confined to the utilitarian morality? Does the belief that moral obligation has its seat outside the mind [p. 230] make the feeling of it too strong to be got rid of? The fact is so far otherwise, that all moralists admit and lament the ease with which, in the generality of minds, conscience can be silenced or stifled. The question, Need I obey my conscience? is quite as often put to themselves by persons who never heard of the principle of utility, as by its adherents. Those whose conscientious feelings are so weak as to allow of their asking this question, if they answer it affirmatively, will not do so because they believe in the transcendental theory, but because of the external sanctions.

It is not necessary, for the present purpose, to decide whether the feeling of duty is innate or implanted. Assuming it to be innate, it is an open question to what objects it naturally attaches itself; for the philosophic supporters of that theory are now agreed that the intuitive perception is of principles of morality, and not of the details. If there be anything innate in the matter, I see no reason why the feeling which is innate should not be that of regard to the pleasures and pains of others. If there is any principle of morals which is intuitively obligatory, I should say it must be that. If so, the intuitive ethics would coincide with the utilitarian, and there would be no further quarrel between them. Even as it is, the intuitive moralists, though they believe that there are other intuitive moral obligations, do already believe this to be one; for they unanimously hold that a large *portion* of morality turns upon the consideration due to the interests of our fellow creatures. Therefore, if the belief in the transcendental origin of

III.7

moral obligation gives any additional efficacy to the internal sanction, it appears to me that the utilitarian principle has already the benefit of it.

III.8   On the other hand, if, as is my own belief, the moral feelings are not innate, but acquired, they are not for that reason the less natural. It is natural to man to speak, to reason, to build cities, to cultivate the ground, though these are acquired faculties. The moral feelings are not indeed a part of our nature, in the sense of being in any perceptible degree present in all of us; but this, unhappily, is a fact admitted by those who believe the most strenuously in their transcendental origin. Like the other acquired capacities above referred to, the moral faculty, if not a part of our nature, is a natural outgrowth from it; capable, like them, in a certain small degree, of springing up spontaneously; and susceptible of being brought by cultivation to a high degree of development. Unhappily it is also susceptible, by a sufficient use of the external sanctions and of the force of early impressions, of being cultivated in almost any direction: so that there is hardly anything so absurd or so mischievous that it may not, by means of these influences, be made to act on the human mind with all the authority of conscience. To doubt that the same potency might be given by the same means to the principle of utility, even if it had no foundation in human nature, would be flying in the face of all experience.

III.9   But moral associations which are wholly of artificial creation, when intellectual culture goes on, yield by degrees to the dissolving force of analysis:[3] [p. 231] and if the feeling of duty, when associated with utility, would appear equally arbitrary; if there were no leading department of our nature, no powerful class of sentiments, with which that association would harmonize, which would make us feel it congenial, and incline us not only to foster it in others (for which we have abundant interested motives), but also to cherish it in ourselves; if there were not, in short, a natural basis of sentiment for utilitarian morality, it might well happen that this association also, even after it had been implanted by education, might be analysed away.

III.10   But there *is* this basis of powerful natural sentiment; and this it is which, when once the general happiness is recognised as the ethical standard, will constitute the strength of the utilitarian morality. This firm foundation is that of the social feelings of mankind; the desire to be in unity with our fellow creatures, which is already a powerful principle in human nature, and happily one of those which tend to become stronger, even without express inculcation, from the influences of advancing civilization. The social state is at once so natural, so necessary, and so habitual to man, that, except in some unusual circumstances or by an effort of voluntary abstraction, he never conceives himself otherwise than as a member of a body; and this association is riveted more and more, as mankind are further removed from the state of savage independence. Any condition, therefore, which is essential to a state of society, becomes more and more an inseparable part of every person's conception of the state of things which he is born into, and which is the destiny of a human being. Now, society between human beings, except in the relation of master and slave, is manifestly impossible on any other footing than that the interests of all are to be consulted. Society between equals can only exist on the understanding that the interests of all are to be regarded equally. And since in all states of civilization, every person, except an absolute monarch, has equals, every one is obliged to live on these terms with somebody; and in every age some advance is made towards a state in which it will be impossible to live permanently on other terms with anybody. In this way people grow up unable to conceive as possible to them a state of total disregard of other people's interests. They are under a necessity of conceiving themselves as at least abstaining from all the grosser injuries, and (if only for their own protection) living in a state of constant protest against them. They are also familiar with the fact of co-operating with others, and proposing to themselves a collective, not an individual, interest, as the aim (at least for the time being) of their actions. So long as they are co-operating, their ends are identified with those of others; there is at least a temporary feeling that the interests of others are their own interests. Not only does all strengthening of social ties, and all healthy growth of society, give to each individual a stronger personal interest in practically consulting the welfare of others; it also leads him to identify his *feelings* more and more with their good, or at least with an ever greater degree of practical consideration for it. [p. 232] He comes, as though instinctively, to be conscious of himself as a being who *of course* pays regard to others. The good of others becomes to him a thing naturally and necessarily to be attended to, like any of the physical conditions of our existence. Now, whatever amount of this feeling a person has, he is urged by the strongest motives both of interest and of sympathy to demonstrate it, and to the utmost of his power encourage it in others; and even

if he has none of it himself, he is as greatly interested as any one else that others should have it. Consequently, the smallest germs of the feeling are laid hold of and nourished by the contagion of sympathy and the influences of education; and a complete web of corroborative association is woven round it, by the powerful agency of the external sanctions. This mode of conceiving ourselves and human life, as civilization goes on, is felt to be more and more natural. Every step in political improvement renders it more so, by removing the sources of opposition of interest, and levelling those inequalities of legal privilege between individuals or classes, owing to which there are large portions of mankind whose happiness it is still practicable to disregard. In an improving state of the human mind, the influences are constantly on the increase, which tend to generate in each individual a feeling of unity with all the rest; which feeling, if perfect, would make him never think of, or desire, any beneficial condition for himself, in the benefits of which they are not included. If we now suppose this feeling of unity to be taught as a religion, and the whole force of education, of institutions, and of opinion, directed, as it once was in the case of religion, to make every person grow up from infancy surrounded on all sides both by the profession and by the practice of it, I think that no one, who can realize this conception, will feel any misgiving about the sufficiency of the ultimate sanction for the Happiness morality. To any ethical student who finds the realization difficult, I recommend, as a means of facilitating it, the second of M. Comte's two principal works, the *Système de Politique Positive*. I entertain the strongest objections to the system of politics and morals set forth in that treatise; but I think it has superabundantly shown the possibility of giving to the service of humanity, even without the aid of belief in a Providence, both the psychical power and the social efficacy of a religion; making it take hold of human life, and colour all thought, feeling, and action, in a manner of which the greatest ascendancy ever exercised by any religion may be but a type and foretaste; and of which the danger is, not that it should be insufficient, but that it should be so excessive as to interfere unduly with human freedom and individuality.[4]
[p. 233]

III.11   Neither is it necessary to the feeling which constitutes the binding force of the utilitarian morality on those who recognise it, to wait for those social influences which would make its obligation felt by mankind at large. In the comparatively early state of human advancement in which we now live, a person cannot indeed feel that entireness of sympathy with all others, which would make any real discordance in the general direction of their conduct in life impossible; but already a person in whom the social feeling is at all developed, cannot bring himself to think of the rest of his fellow creatures as struggling rivals with him for the means of happiness, whom he must desire to see defeated in their object in order that he may succeed in his. The deeply-rooted conception which every individual even now has of himself as a social being, tends to make him feel it one of his natural wants that there should be harmony between his feelings and aims and those of his fellow creatures. If differences of opinion and of mental culture make it impossible for him to share many of their actual feelings— perhaps make him denounce and defy those feelings—he still needs to be conscious that his real aim and theirs do not conflict; that he is not opposing himself to what they really wish for, namely, their own good, but is, on the contrary, promoting it. This feeling in most individuals is much inferior in strength to their selfish feelings, and is often wanting altogether. But to those who have it, it possesses all the characters of a natural feeling. It does not present itself to their minds as a superstition of education, or a law despotically imposed by the power of society, but as an attribute which it would not be well for them to be without. This conviction is the ultimate sanction of the greatest-happiness morality. This it is which makes any mind, of well-developed feelings, work with, and not against, the outward motives to care for others, afforded by what I have called the external sanctions; and when those sanctions are wanting, or act in an opposite direction, constitutes in itself a powerful internal binding force, in proportion to the sensitiveness and thoughtfulness of the character; since few but those whose mind is a moral blank, could bear to lay out their course of life on the plan of paying no regard to others except so far as their own private interest compels.

Chapter III Endnotes

1. In the penultimate sentence of paragraph III.4, the phrase "mass of feeling which must be broken through" suggests an important aspect of Mill's conception of the influence of conscience:

namely, that it can cause pain in advance of action, not just afterward. Mill had previously stated this more explicitly in "Remarks on Bentham's Philosophy" (1833, CW vol. X, p. 12):

> The pain or pleasure which determines our conduct is as frequently one which *precedes* the moment of action as one which follows it. [. . .] the case *may* be, and is to the full as likely to be, that he recoils from the very thought of committing the act; the idea of placing himself in such a situation is so painful, that he cannot dwell upon it long enough to have even the physical power of perpetrating the crime. His conduct is determined by pain; but by a pain which precedes the act, not by one which is expected to follow it.

2. In paragraph III.5, Mill claims that utilitarianism can be supported by a person's conscience as strongly as any other moral standard can. This can be seen as part of a broader agenda of establishing that conscience and other traditional moral notions are perfectly at home within utilitarianism, not displaced by it. This agenda is also pursued in "Whewell on Moral Philosophy" (1852, CW vol. X, p. 172):

> He [Whewell] appropriates to his own side of the question all the expressions, such as conscience, duty, rectitude, with which the reverential feelings of mankind towards moral ideas are associated, and cries out, *I* am for these noble things, *you* are for pleasure, or utility. We cannot accept this as a description of the matter in issue. Dr. Whewell is assuming to himself what belongs quite as rightfully to his antagonists. We are as much for conscience, duty, rectitude, as Dr. Whewell. The terms, and all the feelings connected with them, are as much a part of the ethics of utility as of that of intuition.

3. In the first sentence of paragraph III.9, Mill refers to the "dissolving force of analysis." His *Autobiography* provides an illustration of this phenomenon, based on what he called a "crisis in my mental history" at the age of twenty (1873, CW vol. I, p. 141 and p. 143):

> [. . .] I now saw, or thought I saw, what I had always before received with incredulity—that the habit of analysis has a

tendency to wear away the feelings [. . .]. The very excellence of analysis (I argued) is that it tends to weaken and undermine whatever is the result of prejudice; that it enables us mentally to separate ideas which have only casually clung together: and no associations whatever could ultimately resist this dissolving force [. . .]. [p. 143] All those to whom I looked up, were of opinion that the pleasure of sympathy with human beings, and the feelings which made the good of others, and especially of mankind on a large scale, the object of existence, were the greatest and surest sources of happiness. Of the truth of this I was convinced, but to know that a feeling would make me happy if I had it, did not give me the feeling. My education, I thought, had failed to create these feelings in sufficient strength to resist the dissolving influence of analysis, while the whole course of my intellectual cultivation had made precocious and premature analysis the inveterate habit of my mind.

4. In paragraph III.10, Mill claims that utilitarian morality is insulated from the "dissolving force of analysis" (as he called it in paragraph III.9) by "the social feelings of mankind." Mill expressed similar ideas, albeit in a more preliminary way, in his letter to William George Ward (1859, CW vol. XV, pp. 649–50):

> I conceive that feeling [i.e., moral feeling] to be a natural outgrowth from the social nature of man: a [p. 650] state of society is so eminently natural to human beings that anything which is an obviously indispensable condition of social life, easily comes to act upon their minds almost like a physical necessity. Now it is an indispensable condition of all society, except between master & slave, that each shall pay regard to the other's happiness. On this basis, combined with a human creature's capacity of *fellow-feeling*, the feelings of morality properly so called seem to me to be grounded, & their main constituent to be the idea of punishment. I feel conscious that if I violate certain laws, other people must necessarily or naturally desire that I sh^d be punished for the violation. I also feel that I sh^d desire them to be punished if they violated the same laws towards me.

Chapter IV: Of What Sort of Proof the Principle of Utility Is Susceptible

IV.1   It has already been remarked, that questions of ultimate ends do not admit of proof, in the ordinary acceptation of the term. To be incapable of proof by reasoning is common to all first principles; to the first premises of our knowledge, as well as to those of our conduct. But the former, being matters of fact, may be the subject of a direct appeal to the faculties which judge of fact—namely, our senses, and our internal consciousness. Can an appeal be made to the same faculties on questions of practical ends? Or by what other faculty is cognizance taken of them?

IV.2   Questions about ends are, in other words, questions what things are desirable. The utilitarian doctrine is, that happiness is desirable, and the only thing desirable, as an end; all other things being only desirable as means to that end. What ought to be required of this doctrine—what conditions is it requisite that the doctrine should fulfil—to make good its claim to be believed?

IV.3   The only proof capable of being given that an object is visible, is that people actually see it. The only proof that a sound is audible, is that people hear it: and so of the other sources of our experience. In like manner, I apprehend, the sole evidence it is possible to produce that anything is desirable, is that people do actually desire it. If the end which the utilitarian doctrine proposes to itself were not, in theory and in practice, acknowledged to be an end, nothing could ever convince any person that it was so. No reason can be given why the general happiness is desirable, except that each person, so far as he believes it to be attainable, desires his own happiness. This, however, being a fact, we have not only all the proof which the case admits of, but all which it is possible to require, that happiness is a good: that each person's happiness is a good to that person, and the general happiness, therefore, a good to the aggregate of all persons.[1] Happiness has made out its title as *one* of the ends of conduct, and consequently one of the criteria of morality.

But it has not, by this alone, proved itself to be the sole criterion. To do that, it would seem, by the same rule, necessary to show, not only that people desire happiness, but that they never desire anything else. Now it is palpable [p. 235] that they do desire things which, in common language, are decidedly distinguished from happiness. They desire, for example, virtue, and the absence of vice, no less really than pleasure and the absence of pain. The desire of virtue is not as universal, but it is as authentic a fact, as the desire of happiness. And hence the opponents of the utilitarian standard deem that they have a right to infer that there are other ends of human action besides happiness, and that happiness is not the standard of approbation and disapprobation.

IV.4

But does the utilitarian doctrine deny that people desire virtue, or maintain that virtue is not a thing to be desired? The very reverse. It maintains not only that virtue is to be desired, but that it is to be desired disinterestedly, for itself. Whatever may be the opinion of utilitarian moralists as to the original conditions by which virtue is made virtue; however they may believe (as they do) that actions and dispositions are only virtuous because they promote another end than virtue; yet this being granted, and it having been decided, from considerations of this description, what *is* virtuous, they not only place virtue at the very head of the things which are good as means to the ultimate end, but they also recognise as a psychological fact the possibility of its being, to the individual, a good in itself, without looking to any end beyond it; and hold, that the mind is not in a right state, not in a state conformable to Utility, not in the state most conducive to the general happiness, unless it does love virtue in this manner—as a thing desirable in itself, even although, in the individual instance, it should not produce those other desirable consequences which it tends to produce, and on account of which it is held to be virtue. This opinion is not, in the smallest degree, a departure from the Happiness principle. The ingredients of happiness are very various, and each of them is desirable in itself, and not merely when considered as swelling an aggregate. The principle of utility does not mean that any given pleasure, as music, for instance, or any given exemption from pain, as for example health, are to be looked upon as means to a collective something termed happiness, and to be desired on that account. They are desired and desirable in and for themselves; besides being means, they are a part of the end. Virtue, according to the utilitarian doctrine, is not naturally and originally part of the end, but it is capable of

IV.5

becoming so; and in those who love it disinterestedly it has become so, and is desired and cherished, not as a means to happiness, but as a part of their happiness.

IV.6   To illustrate this farther, we may remember that virtue is not the only thing, originally a means, and which if it were not a means to anything else, would be and remain indifferent, but which by association with what it is a means to, comes to be desired for itself, and that too with the utmost intensity. What, for example, shall we say of the love of money? There is nothing originally more desirable about money than about any heap of glittering [p. 236] pebbles. Its worth is solely that of the things which it will buy; the desires for other things than itself, which it is a means of gratifying. Yet the love of money is not only one of the strongest moving forces of human life, but money is, in many cases, desired in and for itself; the desire to possess it is often stronger than the desire to use it, and goes on increasing when all the desires which point to ends beyond it, to be compassed by it, are falling off. It may be then said truly, that money is desired not for the sake of an end, but as part of the end. From being a means to happiness, it has come to be itself a principal ingredient of the individual's conception of happiness. The same may be said of the majority of the great objects of human life—power, for example, or fame; except that to each of these there is a certain amount of immediate pleasure annexed, which has at least the semblance of being naturally inherent in them; a thing which cannot be said of money. Still, however, the strongest natural attraction, both of power and of fame, is the immense aid they give to the attainment of our other wishes; and it is the strong association thus generated between them and all our objects of desire, which gives to the direct desire of them the intensity it often assumes, so as in some characters to surpass in strength all other desires. In these cases the means have become a part of the end, and a more important part of it than any of the things which they are means to. What was once desired as an instrument for the attainment of happiness, has come to be desired for its own sake. In being desired for its own sake it is, however, desired as *part* of happiness. The person is made, or thinks he would be made, happy by its mere possession; and is made unhappy by failure to obtain it. The desire of it is not a different thing from the desire of happiness, any more than the love of music, or the desire of health. They are included in happiness. They are some of the elements of which the desire of happiness is made up. Happiness is not

an abstract idea, but a concrete whole; and these are some of its parts. ✗
And the utilitarian standard sanctions and approves their being so. Life
would be a poor thing, very ill provided with sources of happiness,
if there were not this provision of nature, by which things originally
indifferent, but conducive to, or otherwise associated with, the satisfaction of our primitive desires, become in themselves sources of pleasure more valuable than the primitive pleasures, both in permanency,
in the space of human existence that they are capable of covering, and
even in intensity.[2]

Virtue, according to the utilitarian conception, is a good of this   IV.7
description. There was no original desire of it, or motive to it, save its
conduciveness to pleasure, and especially to protection from pain. But
through the association thus formed, it may be felt a good in itself,
and desired as such with as great intensity as any other good; and with
this difference between it and the [p. 237] love of money, of power,
or of fame, that all of these may, and often do, render the individual
noxious to the other members of the society to which he belongs,
whereas there is nothing which makes him so much a blessing to them
as the cultivation of the disinterested love of virtue. And consequently,
the utilitarian standard, while it tolerates and approves those other
acquired desires, up to the point beyond which they would be more
injurious to the general happiness than promotive of it, enjoins and
requires the cultivation of the love of virtue up to the greatest strength
possible, as being above all things important to the general happiness.

It results from the preceding considerations, that there is in reality   IV.8
nothing desired except happiness. Whatever is desired otherwise than
as a means to some end beyond itself, and ultimately to happiness, is
desired as itself a part of happiness, and is not desired for itself until
it has become so. Those who desire virtue for its own sake, desire it
either because the consciousness of it is a pleasure, or because the
consciousness of being without it is a pain, or for both reasons united;
as in truth the pleasure and pain seldom exist separately, but almost
always together, the same person feeling pleasure in the degree of virtue attained, and pain in not having attained more. If one of these gave
him no pleasure, and the other no pain, he would not love or desire
virtue, or would desire it only for the other benefits which it might
produce to himself or to persons whom he cared for.

We have now, then, an answer to the question, of what sort of proof   IV.9
the principle of utility is susceptible. If the opinion which I have now

stated is psychologically true—if human nature is so constituted as to desire nothing which is not either a part of happiness or a means of happiness, we can have no other proof, and we require no other, that these are the only things desirable. If so, happiness is the sole end of human action, and the promotion of it the test by which to judge of all human conduct; from whence it necessarily follows that it must be the criterion of morality, since a part is included in the whole.

IV.10   And now to decide whether this is really so; whether mankind do desire nothing for itself but that which is a pleasure to them, or of which the absence is a pain; we have evidently arrived at a question of fact and experience, dependent, like all similar questions, upon evidence. It can only be determined by practised self-consciousness and self-observation, assisted by observation of others. I believe that these sources of evidence, impartially consulted, will declare that desiring a thing and finding it pleasant, aversion to it and thinking of it as painful, are phenomena entirely inseparable, or rather two parts of the same phenomenon; in strictness of language, two different modes of naming the same psychological fact: that to think of an object as desirable (unless for the sake of its consequences), and to think of it as [p. 238] pleasant, are one and the same thing; and that to desire anything, except in proportion as the idea of it is pleasant, is a physical and metaphysical impossibility.

IV.11   So obvious does this appear to me, that I expect it will hardly be disputed: and the objection made will be, not that desire can possibly be directed to anything ultimately except pleasure and exemption from pain, but that the will is a different thing from desire; that a person of confirmed virtue, or any other person whose purposes are fixed, carries out his purposes without any thought of the pleasure he has in contemplating them, or expects to derive from their fulfilment; and persists in acting on them, even though these pleasures are much diminished, by changes in his character or decay of his passive sensibilities, or are outweighed by the pains which the pursuit of the purposes may bring upon him. All this I fully admit, and have stated it elsewhere, as positively and emphatically as any one.[3] Will, the active phenomenon, is a different thing from desire, the state of passive sensibility, and though originally an offshoot from it, may in time take root and detach itself from the parent stock; so much so, that in the case of an habitual purpose, instead of willing the thing because we desire it, we often desire it only because we will it. This, however, is but an

instance of that familiar fact, the power of habit, and is nowise confined to the case of virtuous actions. Many indifferent things, which
men originally did from a motive of some sort, they continue to do
from habit. Sometimes this is done unconsciously, the consciousness
coming only after the action: at other times with conscious volition,
but volition which has became habitual, and is put into operation by
the force of habit, in opposition perhaps to the deliberate preference,
as often happens with those who have contracted habits of vicious
or hurtful indulgence. Third and last comes the case in which the
habitual act of will in the individual instance is not in contradiction to
the general intention prevailing at other times, but in fulfilment of it;
as in the case of the person of confirmed virtue, and of all who pursue deliberately and consistently any determinate end. The distinction
between will and desire thus understood, is an authentic and highly
important psychological fact; but the fact consists solely in this—
that will, like all other parts of our constitution, is amenable to habit,
and that we may will from habit what we no longer desire for itself,
or desire only because we will it. It is not the less true that will, in
the beginning, is entirely produced by desire; including in that term
the repelling influence of pain as well as the attractive one of pleasure. Let us take into consideration, no longer the person who has a
confirmed will to do right, but him in whom that virtuous will is still
feeble, conquerable by temptation, and not to be [p. 239] fully relied
on; by what means can it be strengthened? How can the will to be
virtuous, where it does not exist in sufficient force, be implanted or
awakened? Only by making the person *desire* virtue—by making him
think of it in a pleasurable light, or of its absence in a painful one. It is
by associating the doing right with pleasure, or the doing wrong with
pain, or by eliciting and impressing and bringing home to the person's
experience the pleasure naturally involved in the one or the pain in
the other, that it is possible to call forth that will to be virtuous, which,
when confirmed, acts without any thought of either pleasure or pain.
Will is the child of desire, and passes out of the dominion of its parent only to come under that of habit. That which is the result of habit
affords no presumption of being intrinsically good; and there would
be no reason for wishing that the purpose of virtue should become
independent of pleasure and pain, were it not that the influence of
the pleasurable and painful associations which prompt to virtue is not
sufficiently to be depended on for unerring constancy of action until

it has acquired the support of habit. Both in feeling and in conduct, habit is the only thing which imparts certainty; and it is because of the importance to others of being able to rely absolutely on one's feelings and conduct, and to oneself of being able to rely on one's own, that the will to do right ought to be cultivated into this habitual independence. In other words, this state of the will is a means to good, not intrinsically a good; and does not contradict the doctrine that nothing is a good to human beings but in so far as it is either itself pleasurable, or a means of attaining pleasure or averting pain.

IV.12   But if this doctrine be true, the principle of utility is proved. Whether it is so or not, must now be left to the consideration of the thoughtful reader.

Chapter IV Endnotes

1.   In the penultimate sentence of paragraph IV.3, Mill claims that the general happiness is a good to the aggregate of all persons. Mill commented on this claim in his letter to Henry Jones (1868, CW vol. XVI, p. 1414):

> As to the sentence you quote from my "Utilitarianism"; when I said that the general happiness is a good to the aggregate of all persons I did not mean that every human being's happiness is a good to every other human being; though I think, in a good state of society & education it would be so. I merely meant in this particular sentence to argue that since A's happiness is a good, B's a good, C's a good, &c., the sum of all these goods must be a good.

2.   Paragraph IV.6 contains psychological claims that align with remarks Mill made in two other works.

>   a.   From "Whewell on Moral Philosophy" (1852, CW vol. X, p. 184, fn.):

> > [...] what we desire unselfishly must first, by a mental process, become an actual part of what we seek as our own happiness; [...] the good of others becomes our pleasure because we

have learnt to find pleasure in it: this is, we think, the true philosophical account of the matter.

b. From *James Mill's Analysis of the Phenomena of the Human Mind* (1869, CW vol. XXXI, pp. 231–32):

[. . .] Wealth, Power, Dignity, and many other things which are not in their own nature pleasures, but only causes of pleasures and of exemption from pains, become so closely associated with the pleasures of which they are causes, and their absence or loss becomes so closely associated with the pains to which it exposes us, that the things become objects of [p. 232] love and desire, and their absence an object of hatred and aversion, for their own sake, without reference to their consequences.

3. In the second sentence of paragraph IV.11, Mill refers to having stated some points "elsewhere, as positively and emphatically as any one." He appears to be referring to these remarks from *A System of Logic* (1843, CW vol. VIII, pp. 842–43):

As we proceed in the formation of habits, and become accustomed to will a particular act or a particular course of conduct because it is pleasurable, we at last continue to will it without any reference to its being pleasurable. Although, from some change in us or in our circumstances, we have ceased to find any pleasure in the action, or perhaps to anticipate any pleasure as the consequence of it, we still continue to desire the action, and consequently to do it. In this manner it is that habits of hurtful excess continue to be practised although they have ceased to be pleasurable; and in this manner also it is that the habit of willing to persevere in the course which he has chosen, does not desert the moral hero, even when the reward, however real, which he doubtless receives from the consciousness of well-doing, is anything but an equivalent for the sufferings he undergoes, or the wishes which he may have to renounce.

A habit of willing is commonly called a purpose; and among the causes of our volitions, and of the actions which flow from them, must be reckoned not only likings and aversions, but also purposes. It is only when our pur- [p. 843] poses have become independent of the feelings of pain or pleasure from which they originally took their rise, that we are said to have a confirmed character. "A character," says Novalis, "is a completely fashioned will:" and the will, once so fashioned, may be steady and constant, when the passive susceptibilities of pleasure and pain are greatly weakened, or materially changed.

Chapter V: On the Connexion between Justice and Utility

In all ages of speculation, one of the strongest obstacles to the reception of the doctrine that Utility or Happiness is the criterion of right and wrong, has been drawn from the idea of Justice. The powerful sentiment, and apparently clear perception, which that word recals with a rapidity and certainty resembling an instinct, have seemed to the majority of thinkers to point to an inherent quality in things; to show that the Just must have an existence in Nature as something absolute—generically distinct from every variety of the Expedient, and, in idea, opposed to it, though (as is commonly acknowledged) never, in the long run, disjoined from it in fact. V.1

In the case of this, as of our other moral sentiments, there is no necessary connexion between the question of its origin, and that of its binding force. That a feeling is bestowed on us by Nature, does not necessarily legitimate all its promptings. The feeling of justice might be a peculiar instinct, and might yet require, like our other instincts, to be controlled and enlightened by a higher reason. If we have intellectual instincts, leading us to judge in a particular way, as well as animal instincts that prompt us to act in a particular way, there is no necessity that the former should be more infallible in their sphere than the latter in theirs: it may as well happen that wrong judgments are occasionally suggested by those, as wrong actions by these. But though it is one thing to believe that we have natural feelings of justice, and another to acknowledge them as an ultimate criterion of conduct, these two opinions are very closely connected in point of fact. Mankind are always predisposed to believe that any subjective feeling, not otherwise accounted for, is a revelation of some objective reality. Our present object is to determine whether the reality, to which the feeling of justice corresponds, is one which needs any such special revelation; whether the justice or injustice of an action is a thing intrinsically peculiar, and distinct from all its other qualities, or only a combination of certain of those qualities, presented under a peculiar aspect. For the purpose of this inquiry, it is V.2

practically important to consider whether the feeling itself, of justice and injustice, is *sui generis* like our sensations of colour and taste, or a derivative feeling, formed by a combina- [p. 241] tion of others. And this it is the more essential to examine, as people are in general willing enough to allow, that objectively the dictates of justice coincide with a part of the field of General Expediency; but inasmuch as the subjective mental feeling of Justice is different from that which commonly attaches to simple expediency, and, except in extreme cases of the latter, is far more imperative in its demands, people find it difficult to see, in Justice, only a particular kind or branch of general utility, and think that its superior binding force requires a totally different origin.

V.3   To throw light upon this question, it is necessary to attempt to ascertain what is the distinguishing character of justice, or of injustice: what is the quality, or whether there is any quality, attributed in common to all modes of conduct designated as unjust (for justice, like many other moral attributes, is best defined by its opposite), and distinguishing them from such modes of conduct as are disapproved, but without having that particular epithet of disapprobation applied to them. If, in everything which men are accustomed to characterize as just or unjust, some one common attribute or collection of attributes is always present, we may judge whether this particular attribute or combination of attributes would be capable of gathering round it a sentiment of that peculiar character and intensity by virtue of the general laws of our emotional constitution, or whether the sentiment is inexplicable, and requires to be regarded as a special provision of Nature. If we find the former to be the case, we shall, in resolving this question, have resolved also the main problem: if the latter, we shall have to seek for some other mode of investigating it.

V.4   To find the common attributes of a variety of objects, it is necessary to begin by surveying the objects themselves in the concrete. Let us therefore advert successively to the various modes of action, and arrangements of human affairs, which are classed, by universal or widely spread opinion, as Just or as Unjust. The things well known to excite the sentiments associated with those names, are of a very multifarious character. I shall pass them rapidly in review, without studying any particular arrangement.

V.5   In the first place, it is mostly considered unjust to deprive any one of his personal liberty, his property, or any other thing which belongs to him by law. Here, therefore, is one instance of the application of the terms just and unjust in a perfectly definite sense, namely, that it is just to respect, unjust to violate, the *legal rights* of any one. But this judgment admits of several exceptions, arising from the other forms in which the notions of justice and injustice present themselves. For example, the person who suffers the deprivation may (as the phrase is) have *forfeited* the rights which he is so deprived of: [p. 242] a case to which we shall return presently. But also,

Secondly; the legal rights of which he is deprived, may be rights which *ought* not to have belonged to him; in other words, the law which confers on him these rights, may be a bad law. When it is so, or when (which is the same thing for our purpose) it is supposed to be so, opinions will differ as to the justice or injustice of infringing it. Some maintain that no law, however bad, ought to be disobeyed by an individual citizen; that his opposition to it, if shown at all, should only be shown in endeavouring to get it altered by competent authority. This opinion (which condemns many of the most illustrious benefactors of mankind, and would often protect pernicious institutions against the only weapons which, in the state of things existing at the time, have any chance of succeeding against them) is defended, by those who hold it, on grounds of expediency; principally on that of the importance, to the common interest of mankind, of maintaining inviolate the sentiment of submission to law. Other persons, again, hold the directly contrary opinion, that any law, judged to be bad, may blamelessly be disobeyed, even though it be not judged to be unjust, but only inexpedient; while others would confine the licence of disobedience to the case of unjust laws: but again, some say, that all laws which are inexpedient are unjust; since every law imposes some restriction on the natural liberty of mankind, which restriction is an injustice, unless legitimated by tending to their good. Among these diversities of opinion, it seems to be universally admitted that there may be unjust laws, and that law, consequently, is not the ultimate criterion of justice, but may give to one person a benefit, or impose on another an evil, which justice condemns. When, however, a law is thought to be unjust, it seems always to be regarded as being so in the same way in which a breach of law is unjust, namely, by infringing somebody's right; which, as it cannot in this case be a legal right, receives a different appellation, and is called a moral right. We may say, therefore, that a second case of injustice consists in taking or withholding from any person that to which he has a *moral right*.

V.6

V.7   Thirdly, it is universally considered just that each person should
obtain that (whether good or evil) which he _deserves;_ and unjust that
he should obtain a good, or be made to undergo an evil, which he
does not deserve. This is, perhaps, the clearest and most emphatic form
in which the idea of justice is conceived by the general mind. As
it involves the notion of desert, the question arises, what constitutes
desert? Speaking in a general way, a person is understood to deserve
good if he does right, evil if he does wrong; and in a more particular
sense, to deserve good from those to whom he does or has done good,
and evil from those to whom he does or has done evil. The precept of
returning good for evil has never been regarded as a case of the fulfilment of justice, but as one in which the claims of justice are waved, in
obedience to other considerations.

V.8   Fourthly, it is confessedly unjust to _break faith_ with any one: to violate [p. 243] an engagement, either express or implied, or disappoint
expectations raised by our own conduct, at least if we have raised
those expectations knowingly and voluntarily. Like the other obligations of justice already spoken of, this one is not regarded as absolute,
but as capable of being overruled by a stronger obligation of justice
on the other side; or by such conduct on the part of the person concerned as is deemed to absolve us from our obligation to him, and to
constitute a _forfeiture_ of the benefit which he has been led to expect.

V.9   Fifthly, it is, by universal admission, inconsistent with justice to be
partial; to show favour or preference to one person over another, in matters to which favour and preference do not properly apply. Impartiality,
however, does not seem to be regarded as a duty in itself, but rather as
instrumental to some other duty; for it is admitted that favour and preference are not always censurable, and indeed the cases in which they
are condemned are rather the exception than the rule. A person would
be more likely to be blamed than applauded for giving his family or
friends no superiority in good offices over strangers, when he could do
so without violating any other duty; and no one thinks it unjust to seek
one person in preference to another as a friend, connexion, or companion. Impartiality where rights are concerned is of course obligatory,
but this is involved in the more general obligation of giving to every
one his right. A tribunal, for example, must be impartial, because it is
bound to award, without regard to any other consideration, a disputed
object to the one of two parties who has the right to it. There are other
cases in which impartiality means, being solely influenced by desert;

as with those who, in the capacity of judges, preceptors, or parents, administer reward and punishment as such. There are cases, again, in which it means, being solely influenced by consideration for the public interest; as in making a selection among candidates for a government employment. Impartiality, in short, as an obligation of justice, may be said to mean, being exclusively influenced by the considerations which it is supposed ought to influence the particular case in hand; and resisting the solicitation of any motives which prompt to conduct different from what those considerations would dictate.

Nearly allied to the idea of impartiality, is that of *equality*; which often enters as a component part both into the conception of justice and into the practice of it, and, in the eyes of many persons, constitutes its essence. But in this, still more than in any other case, the notion of justice varies in different persons, and always conforms in its variations to their notion of utility. Each person maintains that equality is the dictate of justice, except where he thinks that expediency requires inequality. The justice of giving equal protection to the rights of all, is maintained by those who support the most outrageous inequality in the rights themselves. Even in slave countries it is theoretically admitted that the rights of the slave, such as they are, ought to be as sacred as those of the master; and that a tribunal which fails to enforce [p. 244] them with equal strictness is wanting in justice; while, at the same time, institutions which leave to the slave scarcely any rights to enforce, are not deemed unjust, because they are not deemed inexpedient. Those who think that utility requires distinctions of rank, do not consider it unjust that riches and social privileges should be unequally dispensed; but those who think this inequality inexpedient, think it unjust also. Whoever thinks that government is necessary, sees no injustice in as much inequality as is constituted by giving to the magistrate powers not granted to other people. Even among those who hold levelling doctrines, there are as many questions of justice as there are differences of opinion about expediency. Some Communists consider it unjust that the produce of the labour of the community should be shared on any other principle than that of exact equality; others think it just that those should receive most whose needs are greatest; while others hold that those who work harder, or who produce more, or whose services are more valuable to the community, may justly claim a larger quota in the division of the produce. And the sense of natural justice may be plausibly appealed to in behalf of every one of these opinions.

V.11   Among so many diverse applications of the term Justice, which yet
is not regarded as ambiguous, it is a matter of some difficulty to seize
the mental link which holds them together, and on which the moral
sentiment adhering to the term essentially depends. Perhaps, in this
embarrassment, some help may be derived from the history of the
word, as indicated by its etymology.

V.12   In most, if not in all, languages, the etymology of the word which
corresponds to Just, points to an origin connected either with positive law, or with that which was in most cases the primitive form of
law—authoritative custom. *Justum* is a form of *jussum*, that which has
been ordered. *Jus* is of the same origin. Δίκαιον comes from δίκη, of
which the principal meaning, at least in the historical ages of Greece,
was a suit at law. Originally, indeed, it meant only the mode or *manner*
of doing things, but it early came to mean the *prescribed* manner; that
which the recognised authorities, patriarchal, judicial, or political,
would enforce. *Recht*, from which came *right* and *righteous*, is synonymous with law. The original meaning indeed of *recht* did not point
to law, but to physical straightness; as *wrong* and its Latin equivalents
meant twisted or *tortuous*; and from this it is argued that right did not
originally mean law, but on the contrary law meant right. But however this may be, the fact that *recht* and *droit* became restricted in their
meaning to positive law, although much which is not required by law
is [p. 245] equally necessary to moral straightness or rectitude, is as
significant of the original character of moral ideas as if the derivation
had been the reverse way. The courts of justice, the administration
of justice, are the courts and the administration of law. *La justice*, in
French, is the established term for judicature. There can, I think, be
no doubt that the *idée mère*, the primitive element, in the formation of
the notion of justice, was conformity to law. It constituted the entire
idea among the Hebrews, up to the birth of Christianity; as might be
expected in the case of a people whose laws attempted to embrace all
subjects on which precepts were required, and who believed those
laws to be a direct emanation from the Supreme Being. But other
nations, and in particular the Greeks and Romans, who knew that
their laws had been made originally, and still continued to be made,
by men, were not afraid to admit that those men might make bad laws;
might do, by law, the same things, and from the same motives, which,
if done by individuals without the sanction of law, would be called
unjust. And hence the sentiment of injustice came to be attached, not

to all violations of law, but only to violations of such laws as *ought* to exist, including such as ought to exist but do not; and to laws themselves, if supposed to be contrary to what ought to be law. In this manner the idea of law and of its injunctions was still predominant in the notion of justice, even when the laws actually in force ceased to be accepted as the standard of it.

It is true that mankind consider the idea of justice and its obliga-   V.13
tions as applicable to many things which neither are, nor is it desired that they should be, regulated by law. Nobody desires that laws should interfere with the whole detail of private life; yet every one allows that in all daily conduct a person may and does show himself to be either just or unjust. But even here, the idea of the breach of what ought to be law, still lingers in a modified shape. It would always give us pleasure, and chime in with our feelings of fitness, that acts which we deem unjust should be punished, though we do not always think it expedient that this should be done by the tribunals. We forego that gratification on account of incidental inconveniences. We should be glad to see just conduct enforced and injustice repressed, even in the minutest details, if we were not, with reason, afraid of trusting the magistrate with so unlimited an amount of power over individuals. When we think that a person is bound in justice to do a thing, it is an ordinary form of language to say, that he ought to be compelled to do it. We should be gratified to see the obligation enforced by anybody who had the power. If we see that its enforcement by law would be inexpedient, we lament the [p. 246] impossibility, we consider the impunity given to injustice as an evil, and strive to make amends for it by bringing a strong expression of our own and the public disapprobation to bear upon the offender. Thus the idea of legal constraint is still the generating idea of the notion of justice, though undergoing several transformations before that notion, as it exists in an advanced state of society, becomes complete.

The above is, I think, a true account, as far as it goes, of the origin and   V.14
progressive growth of the idea of justice. But we must observe, that it contains, as yet, nothing to distinguish that obligation from moral obligation in general. For the truth is, that the idea of penal sanction, which is the essence of law, enters not only into the conception of injustice, but into that of any kind of wrong. We do not call anything wrong, unless we mean to imply that a person ought to be punished in some way or other for doing it; if not by law, by the opinion of his fellow creatures; if

not by opinion, by the reproaches of his own conscience. This seems the real turning point of the distinction between morality and simple expediency.[1] It is a part of the notion of Duty in every one of its forms, that a person may rightfully be compelled to fulfil it. Duty is a thing which may be *exacted* from a person, as one exacts a debt. Unless we think that it might be exacted from him, we do not call it his duty. Reasons of prudence, or the interest of other people, may militate against actually exacting it; but the person himself, it is clearly understood, would not be entitled to complain. There are other things, on the contrary, which we wish that people should do, which we like or admire them for doing, perhaps dislike or despise them for not doing, but yet admit that they are not bound to do; it is not a case of moral obligation; we do not blame them, that is, we do not think that they are proper objects of punishment. How we come by these ideas of deserving and not deserving punishment, will appear, perhaps, in the sequel; but I think there is no doubt that this distinction lies at the bottom of the notions of right and wrong; that we call any conduct wrong, or employ, instead, some other term of dislike or disparagement, according as we think that the person ought, or ought not, to be punished for it; and we say that it would be right to do so and so, or merely that it would be desirable or laudable, according as we would wish to see the person whom it concerns, compelled, or only persuaded and exhorted, to act in that manner.[2]

V.15   This, therefore, being the characteristic difference which marks off, not [p. 247] justice, but morality in general, from the remaining provinces of Expediency and Worthiness; the character is still to be sought which distinguishes justice from other branches of morality. Now it is known that ethical writers divide moral duties into two classes, denoted by the ill-chosen expressions, duties of perfect and of imperfect obligation; the latter being those in which, though the act is obligatory, the particular occasions of performing it are left to our choice; as in the case of charity or beneficence, which we are indeed bound to practise, but not towards any definite person, nor at any prescribed time. In the more precise language of philosophic jurists, duties of perfect obligation are those duties in virtue of which a correlative *right* resides in some person or persons; duties of imperfect

----

[*] See this point enforced and illustrated by Professor Bain, in an admirable chapter (entitled "The Ethical Emotions, or the Moral Sense"), of the second of the two treatises composing his elaborate and profound work on the Mind.

obligation are those moral obligations which do not give birth to any right. I think it will be found that this distinction exactly coincides with that which exists between justice and the other obligations of morality. In our survey of the various popular acceptations of justice, the term appeared generally to involve the idea of a personal right—a claim on the part of one or more individuals, like that which the law gives when it confers a proprietary or other legal right. Whether the injustice consists in depriving a person of a possession, or in breaking faith with him, or in treating him worse than he deserves, or worse than other people who have no greater claims, in each case the supposition implies two things—a wrong done, and some assignable person who is wronged. Injustice may also be done by treating a person better than others; but the wrong in this case is to his competitors, who are also assignable persons. It seems to me that this feature in the case—a right in some person, correlative to the moral obligation—constitutes the specific difference between justice, and generosity or beneficence. Justice implies something which it is not only right to do, and wrong not to do, but which some individual person can claim from us as his moral right. No one has a moral right to our generosity or beneficence, because we are not morally bound to practise those virtues towards any given individual. And it will be found with respect to this as with respect to every correct definition, that the instances which seem to conflict with it are those which most confirm it. For if a moralist attempts, as some have done, to make out that mankind generally, though not any given individual, have a right to all the good we can do them, he at once, by that thesis, includes generosity and beneficence within the category of justice. He is obliged to say, that our utmost exertions are *due* to our fellow creatures, thus assimilating them to a debt; or that nothing less can be a sufficient *return* for what society does for us, thus classing the case as one of gratitude; both of which are acknowledged cases of justice. Wherever there is a right, the case is one of justice, and not of the virtue of beneficence: and whoever does not place the distinction between justice and morality in general where we have now [p. 248] placed it, will be found to make no distinction between them at all, but to merge all morality in justice.

Having thus endeavoured to determine the distinctive elements which enter into the composition of the idea of justice, we are ready to enter on the inquiry, whether the feeling, which accompanies the idea, is attached to it by a special dispensation of nature, or whether it

V.16

could have grown up, by any known laws, out of the idea itself; and in particular, whether it can have originated in considerations of general expediency.

V.17   I conceive that the sentiment itself does not arise from anything which would commonly, or correctly, be termed an idea of expediency; but that though the sentiment does not, whatever is moral in it does.

V.18   We have seen that the two essential ingredients in the sentiment of justice are, the desire to punish a person who has done harm, and the knowledge or belief that there is some definite individual or individuals to whom harm has been done.

V.19   Now it appears to me, that the desire to punish a person who has done harm to some individual, is a spontaneous outgrowth from two sentiments, both in the highest degree natural, and which either are or resemble instincts; the impulse of self-defence, and the feeling of sympathy.

V.20   It is natural to resent, and to repel or retaliate, any harm done or attempted against ourselves, or against those with whom we sympathize. The origin of this sentiment it is not necessary here to discuss. Whether it be an instinct or a result of intelligence, it is, we know, common to all animal nature; for every animal tries to hurt those who have hurt, or who it thinks are about to hurt, itself or its young. Human beings, on this point, only differ from other animals in two particulars. First, in being capable of sympathizing, not solely with their offspring, or, like some of the more noble animals, with some superior animal who is kind to them, but with all human, and even with all sentient, beings. Secondly, in having a more developed intelligence, which gives a wider range to the whole of their sentiments, whether self-regarding or sympathetic. By virtue of his superior intelligence, even apart from his superior range of sympathy, a human being is capable of apprehending a community of interest between himself and the human society of which he forms a part, such that any conduct which threatens the security of the society generally, is threatening to his own, and calls forth his instinct (if instinct it be) of self-defence. The same superiority of intelligence, joined to the power of sympathizing with human beings generally, enables him to attach himself to the collective idea of his tribe, his country, or mankind, in such a manner that any act hurtful to them rouses his instinct of sympathy, and urges him to resistance.

The sentiment of justice, in that one of its elements which consists   V.21
of the [p. 249] desire to punish, is thus, I conceive, the natural feeling of retaliation or vengeance, rendered by intellect and sympathy
applicable to those injuries, that is, to those hurts, which wound us
through, or in common with, society at large. This sentiment, in itself,
has nothing moral in it; what is moral is, the exclusive subordination
of it to the social sympathies, so as to wait on and obey their call. For
the natural feeling tends to make us resent indiscriminately whatever
any one does that is disagreeable to us; but when moralized by the
social feeling, it only acts in the directions conformable to the general
good: just persons resenting a hurt to society, though not otherwise a
hurt to themselves, and not resenting a hurt to themselves, however
painful, unless it be of the kind which society has a common interest
with them in the repression of.

It is no objection against this doctrine to say, that when we feel our   V.22
sentiment of justice outraged, we are not thinking of society at large,
or of any collective interest, but only of the individual case. It is common enough certainly, though the reverse of commendable, to feel
resentment merely because we have suffered pain; but a person whose
resentment is really a moral feeling, that is, who considers whether an
act is blameable before he allows himself to resent it—such a person,
though he may not say expressly to himself that he is standing up for
the interest of society, certainly does feel that he is asserting a rule
which is for the benefit of others as well as for his own. If he is not
feeling this—if he is regarding the act solely as it affects him individually—he is not consciously just; he is not concerning himself about the
justice of his actions. This is admitted even by anti-utilitarian moralists.
When Kant (as before remarked) propounds as the fundamental principle of morals, "So act, that thy rule of conduct might be adopted as a
law by all rational beings," he virtually acknowledges that the interest
of mankind collectively, or at least of mankind indiscriminately, must
be in the mind of the agent when conscientiously deciding on the
morality of the act. Otherwise he uses words without a meaning: for,
that a rule even of utter selfishness could not *possibly* be adopted by all
rational beings—that there is any insuperable obstacle in the nature of
things to its adoption—cannot be even plausibly maintained. To give
any meaning to Kant's principle, the sense put upon it must be, that we
ought to shape our conduct by a rule which all rational beings might
adopt *with benefit to their collective interest.*

V.23   To recapitulate: the idea of justice supposes two things; a rule of conduct, and a sentiment which sanctions the rule. The first must be supposed common to all mankind, and intended for their good. The other (the sentiment) [p. 250] is a desire that punishment may be suffered by those who infringe the rule. There is involved, in addition, the conception of some definite person who suffers by the infringement; whose rights (to use the expression appropriated to the case) are violated by it. And the sentiment of justice appears to me to be, the animal desire to repel or retaliate a hurt or damage to oneself, or to those with whom one sympathizes, widened so as to include all persons, by the human capacity of enlarged sympathy, and the human conception of intelligent self-interest. From the latter elements, the feeling derives its morality; from the former, its peculiar impressiveness, and energy of self-assertion.

V.24   I have, throughout, treated the idea of a *right* residing in the injured person, and violated by the injury, not as a separate element in the composition of the idea and sentiment, but as one of the forms in which the other two elements clothe themselves. These elements are, a hurt to some assignable person or persons on the one hand, and a demand for punishment on the other. An examination of our own minds, I think, will show, that these two things include all that we mean when we speak of violation of a right. When we call anything a person's right, we mean that he has a valid claim on society to protect him in the possession of it, either by the force of law, or by that of education and opinion. If he has what we consider a sufficient claim, on whatever account, to have something guaranteed to him by society, we say that he has a right to it. If we desire to prove that anything does not belong to him by right, we think this done as soon as it is admitted that society ought not to take measures for securing it to him, but should leave it to chance, or to his own exertions. Thus, a person is said to have a right to what he can earn in fair professional competition; because society ought not to allow any other person to hinder him from endeavouring to earn in that manner as much as he can. But he has not a right to three hundred a-year, though he may happen to be earning it; because society is not called on to provide that he shall earn that sum. On the contrary, if he owns ten thousand pounds three per cent stock, he *has* a right to three hundred a-year; because society has come under an obligation to provide him with an income of that amount.

To have a right, then, is, I conceive, to have something which   V.25
society ought to defend me in the possession of. If the objector goes
on to ask why it ought, I can give him no other reason than general
utility.[3] If that expression does not seem to convey a sufficient feeling of the strength of the obligation, nor to account for the peculiar
energy of the feeling, it is because there goes to the composition of
the sentiment, not a rational only but also an animal element, the
thirst for retaliation; and this thirst derives its intensity, as well as its
moral justification, from the extraordinarily important [p. 251] and
impressive kind of utility which is concerned. The interest involved
is that of security, to every one's feelings the most vital of all interests. Nearly all other earthly benefits are needed by one person, not
needed by another; and many of them can, if necessary, be cheer-
fully foregone, or replaced by something else; but security no human
being can possibly do without; on it we depend for all our immunity
from evil, and for the whole value of all and every good, beyond the
passing moment; since nothing but the gratification of the instant
could be of any worth to us, if we could be deprived of everything
the next instant by whoever was momentarily stronger than ourselves. Now this most indispensable of all necessaries, after physical nutriment, cannot be had, unless the machinery for providing it
is kept unintermittedly in active play. Our notion, therefore, of the
claim we have on our fellow-creatures to join in making safe for us
the very groundwork of our existence, gathers feelings round it so
much more intense than those concerned in any of the more common cases of utility, that the difference in degree (as is often the case
in psychology) becomes a real difference in kind. The claim assumes
that character of absoluteness, that apparent infinity, and incommen-
surability with all other considerations, which constitute the distinction between the feeling of right and wrong and that of ordinary
expediency and inexpediency. The feelings concerned are so powerful, and we count so positively on finding a responsive feeling in others (all being alike interested), that *ought* and *should* grow into *must*,
and recognised indispensability becomes a moral necessity, analogous
to physical, and often not inferior to it in binding force.

If the preceding analysis, or something resembling it, be not the   V.26
correct account of the notion of justice; if justice be totally independent of utility, and be a standard *per se*, which the mind can recognise

by simple introspection of itself; it is hard to understand why that internal oracle is so ambiguous, and why so many things appear either just or unjust, according to the light in which they are regarded.

V.27 We are continually informed that Utility is an uncertain standard, which every different person interprets differently, and that there is no safety but in the immutable, ineffaceable, and unmistakeable dictates of Justice, which carry their evidence in themselves, and are independent of the fluctuations of opinion. One would suppose from this that on questions of justice there could be no controversy; that if we take that for our rule, its application to any given case could leave us in as little doubt as a mathematical demonstration. So far is this from being the fact, that there is as much difference of opinion, and as fierce discussion, about what is just, as about what is useful to society. Not only have different nations and individuals different notions [p. 252] of justice, but, in the mind of one and the same individual, justice is not some one rule, principle, or maxim, but many, which do not always coincide in their dictates, and in choosing between which, he is guided either by some extraneous standard, or by his own personal predilections.

V.28 For instance, there are some who say, that it is unjust to punish any one for the sake of example to others; that punishment is just, only when intended for the good of the sufferer himself. Others maintain the extreme reverse, contending that to punish persons who have attained years of discretion, for their own benefit, is despotism and injustice, since if the matter at issue is solely their own good, no one has a right to control their own judgment of it; but that they may justly be punished to prevent evil to others, this being an exercise of the legitimate right of self-defence. Mr. Owen, again, affirms that it is unjust to punish at all; for the criminal did not make his own character; his education, and the circumstances which surround him, have made him a criminal, and for these he is not responsible. All these opinions are extremely plausible; and so long as the question is argued as one of justice simply, without going down to the principles which lie under justice and are the source of its authority, I am unable to see how any of these reasoners can be refuted. For, in truth, every one of the three builds upon rules of justice confessedly true. The first appeals to the acknowledged injustice of singling out an individual, and making him a sacrifice, without his consent, for other people's benefit. The second relies on the acknowledged justice of self-defence, and the admitted injustice of forcing one person to conform to another's notions of what constitutes his good. The Owenite invokes the admitted principle, that it is unjust to punish any one for what he cannot help. Each is triumphant so long as he is not compelled to take into consideration any other maxims of justice than the one he has selected; but as soon as their several maxims are brought face to face, each disputant seems to have exactly as much to say for himself as the others. No one of them can carry out his own notion of justice without trampling upon another equally binding. These are difficulties; they have always been felt to be such; and many devices have been invented to turn rather than to overcome them. As a refuge from the last of the three, men imagined what they called the freedom of the will; fancying that they could not justify punishing a man whose will is in a thoroughly hateful state, unless it be supposed to have come into that state through no influence of anterior circumstances. To escape from the other difficulties, a favourite contrivance has been the fiction of a contract, whereby at some unknown period all the members of society engaged to obey the laws, and consented to be punished for any disobedience to them; thereby giving to their legislators the right, which it is assumed they would not otherwise have had, of punishing them, either for their own good or for [p. 253] that of society. This happy thought was considered to get rid of the whole difficulty, and to legitimate the infliction of punishment, in virtue of another received maxim of justice, *volenti non fit injuria*; that is not unjust which is done with the consent of the person who is supposed to be hurt by it. I need hardly remark, that even if the consent were not a mere fiction, this maxim is not superior in authority to the others which it is brought in to supersede. It is, on the contrary, an instructive specimen of the loose and irregular manner in which supposed principles of justice grow up. This particular one evidently came into use as a help to the coarse exigencies of courts of law, which are sometimes obliged to be content with very uncertain presumptions, on account of the greater evils which would often arise from any attempt on their part to cut finer. But even courts of law are not able to adhere consistently to the maxim, for they allow voluntary engagements to be set aside on the ground of fraud, and sometimes on that of mere mistake or misinformation.

Again, when the legitimacy of inflicting punishment is admitted, how many conflicting conceptions of justice come to light in discussing the proper apportionment of punishment to offences. No rule on this subject recommends itself so strongly to the primitive and

V.29

spontaneous sentiment of justice, as the *lex talionis*, an eye for an eye and a tooth for a tooth. Though this principle of the Jewish and of the Mahomedan law has been generally abandoned in Europe as a practical maxim, there is, I suspect, in most minds, a secret hankering after it; and when retribution accidentally falls on an offender in that precise shape, the general feeling of satisfaction evinced, bears witness how natural is the sentiment to which this repayment in kind is acceptable. With many the test of justice in penal infliction is that the punishment should be proportioned to the offence; meaning that it should be exactly measured by the moral guilt of the culprit (whatever be their standard for measuring moral guilt): the consideration, what amount of punishment is necessary to deter from the offence, having nothing to do with the question of justice, in their estimation: while there are others to whom that consideration is all in all; who maintain that it is not just, at least for man, to inflict on a fellow-creature, whatever may be his offences, any amount of suffering beyond the least that will suffice to prevent him from repeating, and others from imitating, his misconduct.

V.30   To take another example from a subject already once referred to. In a co-operative industrial association, is it just or not that talent or skill should give a title to superior remuneration? On the negative side of the question it is argued, that whoever does the best he can, deserves equally well, and [p. 254] ought not in justice to be put in a position of inferiority for no fault of his own; that superior abilities have already advantages more than enough, in the admiration they excite, the personal influence they command, and the internal sources of satisfaction attending them, without adding to these a superior share of the world's goods; and that society is bound in justice rather to make compensation to the less favoured, for this unmerited inequality of advantages, than to aggravate it. On the contrary side it is contended, that society receives more from the more efficient labourer; that his services being more useful, society owes him a larger return for them; that a greater share of the joint result is actually his work, and not to allow his claim to it is a kind of robbery; that if he is only to receive as much as others, he can only be justly required to produce as much, and to give a smaller amount of time and exertion, proportioned to his superior efficiency. Who shall decide between these appeals to conflicting principles of justice? Justice has in this case two sides to it, which it is impossible to bring into harmony, and the two disputants have chosen opposite sides; the one looks to what it is just that the individual should receive, the other to what it is just that the community should give. Each, from his own point of view, is unanswerable; and any choice between them, on grounds of justice, must be perfectly arbitrary. Social utility alone can decide the preference.

How many, again, and how irreconcileable, are the standards of justice to which reference is made in discussing the repartition of taxation. One opinion is, that payment to the State should be in numerical proportion to pecuniary means. Others think that justice dictates what they term graduated taxation; taking a higher percentage from those who have more to spare. In point of natural justice a strong case might be made for disregarding means altogether, and taking the same absolute sum (whenever it could be got) from every one: as the subscribers to a mess, or to a club, all pay the same sum for the same privileges, whether they can all equally afford it or not. Since the protection (it might be said) of law and government is afforded to, and is equally required by, all, there is no injustice in making all buy it at the same price. It is reckoned justice, not injustice, that a dealer should charge to all customers the same price for the same article, not a price varying according to their means of payment. This doctrine, as applied to taxation, finds no advocates, because it conflicts strongly with men's feelings of humanity and perceptions of social expediency; but the principle of justice which it invokes is as true and as binding as those which can be appealed to against it. Accordingly, it exerts a tacit influence on the line of defence employed for other modes of assessing taxation. People feel obliged to argue that the State does more for the rich than for the poor, as a justification for its taking more from them: [p. 255] though this is in reality not true, for the rich would be far better able to protect themselves, in the absence of law or government, than the poor, and indeed would probably be successful in converting the poor into their slaves. Others, again, so far defer to the same conception of justice, as to maintain that all should pay an equal capitation tax for the protection of their persons (these being of equal value to all), and an unequal tax for the protection of their property, which is unequal. To this others reply, that the all of one man is as valuable to him as the all of another. From these confusions there is no other mode of extrication than the utilitarian.

V.31

Is, then, the difference between the Just and the Expedient a merely imaginary distinction? Have mankind been under a delusion in thinking

V.32

that justice is a more sacred thing than policy, and that the latter ought only to be listened to after the former has been satisfied? By no means. The exposition we have given of the nature and origin of the sentiment, recognises a real distinction; and no one of those who profess the most sublime contempt for the consequences of actions as an element in their morality, attaches more importance to the distinction than I do. While I dispute the pretensions of any theory which sets up an imaginary standard of justice not grounded on utility, I account the justice which is grounded on utility to be the chief part, and incomparably the most sacred and binding part, of all morality. Justice is a name for certain classes of moral rules, which concern the essentials of human well-being more nearly, and are therefore of more absolute obligation, than any other rules for the guidance of life; and the notion which we have found to be of the essence of the idea of justice, that of a right residing in an individual, implies and testifies to this more binding obligation.

V.33   The moral rules which forbid mankind to hurt one another (in which we must never forget to include wrongful interference with each other's freedom) are more vital to human well-being than any maxims, however important, which only point out the best mode of managing some department of human affairs. They have also the peculiarity, that they are the main element in determining the whole of the social feelings of mankind. It is their observance which alone preserves peace among human beings: if obedience to them were not the rule, and disobedience the exception, every one would see in every one else a probable enemy, against whom he must be perpetually guarding himself. What is hardly less important, these are the precepts which mankind have the strongest and the most direct inducements for impressing upon one another. By merely giving to each other prudential instruction or exhortation, they may gain, or think they gain, nothing: in inculcating on each other the duty of positive beneficence they have an unmistakeable interest, but far less in degree: a person may possibly not need the benefits of [p. 256] others; but he always needs that they should not do him hurt. Thus the moralities which protect every individual from being harmed by others, either directly or by being hindered in his freedom of pursuing his own good, are at once those which he himself has most at heart, and those which he has the strongest interest in publishing and enforcing by word and deed. It is by a person's observance of these, that his fitness to exist as one of the fellowship of human beings, is tested and decided; for on that depends his being a nuisance or not to those with whom he is in contact. Now it is these moralities primarily, which compose the obligations of justice. The most marked cases of injustice, and those which give the tone to the feeling of repugnance which characterizes the sentiment, are acts of wrongful aggression, or wrongful exercise of power over some one; the next are those which consist in wrongfully withholding from him something which is his due; in both cases, inflicting on him a positive hurt, either in the form of direct suffering, or of the privation of some good which he had reasonable ground, either of a physical or of a social kind, for counting upon.

The same powerful motives which command the observance of   V.34 these primary moralities, enjoin the punishment of those who violate them; and as the impulses of self-defence, of defence of others, and of vengeance, are all called forth against such persons, retribution, or evil for evil, becomes closely connected with the sentiment of justice, and is universally included in the idea. Good for good is also one of the dictates of justice; and this, though its social utility is evident, and though it carries with it a natural human feeling, has not at first sight that obvious connexion with hurt or injury, which, existing in the most elementary cases of just and unjust, is the source of the characteristic intensity of the sentiment. But the connexion, though less obvious, is not less real. He who accepts benefits, and denies a return of them when needed, inflicts a real hurt, by disappointing one of the most natural and reasonable of expectations, and one which he must at least tacitly have encouraged, otherwise the benefits would seldom have been conferred. The important rank, among human evils and wrongs, of the disappointment of expectation, is shown in the fact that it constitutes the principal criminality of two such highly immoral acts as a breach of friendship and a breach of promise. Few hurts which human beings can sustain are greater, and none wound more, than when that on which they habitually and with full assurance relied, fails them in the hour of need; and few wrongs are greater than this mere withholding of good; none excite more resentment, either in the person suffering, or in a sympathizing spectator. The principle, therefore, of giving to each what they deserve, that is, good for good as well as evil for evil, is not only included within the idea of Justice as we have defined it, but is a proper object of that intensity of sentiment, which places the Just, in human estimation, above the simply Expedient.

[p. 257]

V.35   Most of the maxims of justice current in the world, and commonly
appealed to in its transactions, are simply instrumental to carrying
into effect the principles of justice which we have now spoken of.
That a person is only responsible for what he has done voluntarily,
or could voluntarily have avoided; that it is unjust to condemn any
person unheard; that the punishment ought to be proportioned to the
offence, and the like, are maxims intended to prevent the just principle
of evil for evil from being perverted to the infliction of evil without that justification. The greater part of these common maxims have
come into use from the practice of courts of justice, which have been
naturally led to a more complete recognition and elaboration than was
likely to suggest itself to others, of the rules necessary to enable them
to fulfil their double function, of inflicting punishment when due, and
of awarding to each person his right.

V.36   That first of judicial virtues, impartiality, is an obligation of justice,
partly for the reason last mentioned; as being a necessary condition of
the fulfilment of the other obligations of justice. But this is not the only
source of the exalted rank, among human obligations, of those maxims
of equality and impartiality, which, both in popular estimation and
in that of the most enlightened, are included among the precepts of
justice. In one point of view, they may be considered as corollaries
from the principles already laid down. If it is a duty to do to each
according to his deserts, returning good for good as well as repress-
ing evil by evil, it necessarily follows that we should treat all equally
well (when no higher duty forbids) who have deserved equally well
of us, and that society should treat all equally well who have deserved
equally well of it, that is, who have deserved equally well absolutely.
This is the highest abstract standard of social and distributive justice;
towards which all institutions, and the efforts of all virtuous citizens,
should be made in the utmost possible degree to converge. But this
great moral duty rests upon a still deeper foundation, being a direct
emanation from the first principle of morals, and not a mere logical corollary from secondary or derivative doctrines. It is involved
in the very meaning of Utility, or the Greatest-Happiness Principle.
That principle is a mere form of words without rational significa-
tion, unless one person's happiness, supposed equal in degree (with
the proper allowance made for kind), is counted for exactly as much
as another's. Those conditions being supplied, Bentham's dictum,

"everybody to count for one, nobody for more than one," might be written under the principle of utility as an explanatory commentary.* The equal claim of everybody to [p. 258] happiness in the estimation of the moralist and the legislator, involves an equal claim to all the means of happiness, except in so far as the inevitable conditions of human life, and the general interest, in which that of every individual is included, set limits to the maxim; and those limits ought to be strictly construed. As every other maxim of justice, so this, is by no means applied or held applicable universally; on the contrary, as I have already remarked, it bends to every person's ideas of social expediency. But in whatever case it is deemed applicable at all, it is held

---

*This implication, in the first principle of the utilitarian scheme, of perfect impartiality between persons, is regarded by Mr. Herbert Spencer (in his *Social Statics*) as a disproof of the pretensions of [p. 258] utility to be a sufficient guide to right; since (he says) the principle of utility presupposes the anterior principle, that everybody has an equal right to happiness. It may be more correctly described as supposing that equal amounts of happiness are equally desirable, whether felt by the same or by different persons. This, however, is not a presupposition; not a premise needful to support the principle of utility, but the very principle itself; for what is the principle of utility, if it be not that "happiness" and "desirable" are synonymous terms? If there is any anterior principle implied, it can be no other than this, that the truths of arithmetic are applicable to the valuation of happiness, as of all other measurable quantities.

Mr. Herbert Spencer, in a private communication on the subject of the preceding Note, objects to being considered an opponent of Utilitarianism, and states that he regards happiness as the ultimate end of morality; but deems that end only partially attainable by empirical generalizations from the observed results of conduct, and completely attainable only by deducing, from the laws of life and the conditions of existence, what kinds of action necessarily tend to produce happiness, and what kinds to produce unhappiness. With the exception of the word "necessarily," I have no dissent to express from this doctrine; and (omitting that word) I am not aware that any modern advocate of utilitarianism is of a different opinion. Bentham, certainly, to whom in the *Social Statics* Mr. Spencer particularly referred, is, least of all writers, chargeable with unwillingness to deduce the effect of actions on happiness from the laws of human nature and the universal conditions of human life. The common charge against him is of relying too exclusively upon such deductions, and declining altogether to be bound by the generalizations from specific experience which Mr. Spencer thinks that utilitarians generally confine themselves to. My own opinion (and, as I collect, Mr. Spencer's) is, that in ethics, as in all other branches of scientific study, the consilience of the results of both these processes, each corroborating and verifying the other, is requisite to give to any general proposition the kind and degree of evidence which constitutes scientific proof.

to be the dictate of justice. All persons are deemed to have a *right* to equality of treatment, except when some recognised social expediency requires the reverse. And hence all social inequalities which have ceased to be considered expedient, assume the character not of simple inexpediency, but of injustice, and appear so tyrannical, that people are apt to wonder how they ever could have been tolerated; forgetful that they themselves perhaps tolerate other inequalities under an equally mistaken notion of expediency, the correction of which would make [p. 259] that which they approve seem quite as monstrous as what they have at last learnt to condemn. The entire history of social improvement has been a series of transitions, by which one custom or institution after another, from being a supposed primary necessity of social existence, has passed into the rank of an universally stigmatized injustice and tyranny. So it has been with the distinctions of slaves and freemen, nobles and serfs, patricians and plebeians; and so it will be, and in part already is, with the aristocracies of colour, race, and sex.

V.37   It appears from what has been said, that justice is a name for certain moral requirements, which, regarded collectively, stand higher in the scale of social utility, and are therefore of more paramount obligation, than any others; though particular cases may occur in which some other social duty is so important, as to overrule any one of the general maxims of justice. Thus, to save a life, it may not only be allowable, but a duty, to steal, or take by force, the necessary food or medicine, or to kidnap, and compel to officiate, the only qualified medical practitioner.[4] In such cases, as we do not call anything justice which is not a virtue, we usually say, not that justice must give way to some other moral principle, but that what is just in ordinary cases is, by reason of that other principle, not just in the particular case. By this useful accommodation of language, the character of indefeasibility attributed to justice is kept up, and we are saved from the necessity of maintaining that there can be laudable injustice.

V.38   The considerations which have now been adduced resolve, I conceive, the only real difficulty in the utilitarian theory of morals. It has always been evident that all cases of justice are also cases of expediency: the difference is in the peculiar sentiment which attaches to the former, as contradistinguished from the latter. If this characteristic sentiment has been sufficiently accounted for; if there is no necessity to assume for it any peculiarity of origin; if it is simply the natural feeling of resentment, moralized by being made co-extensive with the demands of social good; and if this feeling not only does but ought to exist in all the classes of cases to which the idea of justice corresponds; that idea no longer presents itself as a stumbling-block to the utilitarian ethics. Justice remains the appropriate name for certain social utilities which are vastly more important, and therefore more absolute and imperative, than any others are as a class (though not more so than others may be in particular cases); and which, therefore, ought to be, as well as naturally are, guarded by a sentiment not only different in degree, but also in kind; distinguished from the milder feeling which attaches to the mere idea of promoting human pleasure or convenience, at once by the more definite nature of its commands, and by the sterner character of its sanctions.

Chapter V Endnotes

1.   In paragraph V.14, Mill refers to "the distinction between morality and simple expediency." This distinction is related to Mill's views on maximization and supererogation (see Appendix B) and his doctrine of the Art of Life (see Appendix C).

2.   Paragraph V.14 also contains several claims about the conceptual connection between wrongness and punishment. Scholars regard these claims as both important and incomplete. Mill addressed this topic in various ways in several other works.

   a.   From Mill's letter to William George Ward (1859, CW vol. XV, pp. 649–50):

   Now as to the still more important subject of the meaning of *ought*. [. . .] I will therefore pass to the case of those who have a true moral feeling, that is, a feeling of pain in the fact of violating a certain rule, quite independently of any expected consequences to themselves. It appears to me that to them the word *ought* means, that if they act otherwise, they shall be punished by this internal, & perfectly disinterested feeling. Unless they would be so punished, or unless they think they

would, any assertion they make to themselves that they ought
so to act seems to me to lose its proper meaning [. . .].

b.   From Mill's letter to Samuel Bailey (1863, CW vol. XV,
     p. 825), explicitly referring to Chapter V of *Utilitarianism*:

I derive most of the peculiar characters of the moral sentiment from the element of vindictiveness which enters
into it.

c.   From "Austin on Jurisprudence" (1863, CW vol. XXI, p. 181):

With the idea of wrong, that of sanction is inseparably bound
up [. . .].

d.   From *An Examination of Sir William Hamilton's Philosophy*
     (1865, CW vol. IX, p. 454):

What is meant by moral responsibility? Responsibility
means punishment. When we are said to have the feeling of
being morally responsible for our actions, the idea of being
punished for them is uppermost in the speaker's mind. But
the feeling of liability to punishment is of two kinds. It may
mean, expectation that if we act in a certain manner, punishment will actually be inflicted upon us, by our fellow creatures or by a Supreme Power. Or it may only mean, knowing
that we shall deserve that infliction.

e.   From *An Examination of Sir William Hamilton's Philosophy*
     (1865, CW vol. IX, p. 462):

If any one thinks that there is justice in the infliction of pur-
poseless suffering; that there is a natural affinity between the
two ideas of guilt and punishment, which makes it intrinsically fitting that wherever there has been guilt, pain should
be inflicted by way of retribution; I acknowledge that I can
find no argument to justify punishment inflicted on this principle. As a legitimate satisfaction to feelings of indignation and
resentment which are on the whole salutary and worthy of

cultivation, I can in certain cases admit it; but here it is still a means to an end.

f.   From *An Examination of Sir William Hamilton's Philosophy* (1865, CW vol. IX, pp. 463–64):

From our earliest childhood, the idea of doing wrong (that is, of doing what is forbidden, or what is injurious to others) and the idea of punishment are presented to our mind together [. . .].This is quite enough to make the spontaneous feelings of mankind regard punishment and a wrongdoer as naturally fitted [p. 464] to each other—as a conjunction appropriate in itself, independently of any consequences. Even Sir W. Hamilton recognises as one of the common sources of error, that "the associations of thought are mistaken for the connexions of existence."

g.   From *James Mill's Analysis of the Phenomena of the Human Mind* (1869, CW vol. XXXI, pp. 241–42):

I have examined this question in the concluding chapter of a short treatise entitled *Utilitarianism*.The subject of the chapter is "the connexion between Justice and Utility." I have there endeavoured to shew what the association is, which exists in the case of what we regard as a duty, but does not exist in the case of what we merely regard as useful, and which gives to the feeling in the former case the strength, the gravity, and pungency, which in the other case it has not.

I believe that the element in the association, which gives this distinguishing character to the feeling, and which constitutes the difference of the antecedents in the two cases, is the idea of Punishment. I mean the association with punishment, not the expectation of it.

No case can be pointed out in which we consider anything as a duty, and any act [p. 242] or omission as immoral or wrong, without regarding the person who commits the wrong and violates the duty as a fit object of punishment. We think that the general good requires that he should be punished, if not by the law, by the displeasure and ill offices of his fellow-creatures: we at any rate feel indignant with him, that is, it would give us pleasure that he should suffer for his misconduct, even if there are preponderant reasons of another kind against inflicting the suffering.

3. The second sentence of paragraph V.25 states that the basis of rights is "general utility." This claim reinforces the most explicitly utilitarian claim that Mill made in *On Liberty* (1859, CW vol. XVIII, p. 224):

> It is proper to state that I forego any advantage which could be derived to my argument from the idea of abstract right, as a thing independent of utility. I regard utility as the ultimate appeal on all ethical questions: but it must be utility in the largest sense, grounded on the permanent interests of man as a progressive being.

4. In paragraph V.37, Mill writes that in some cases "it may not only be allowable, but a duty, to steal, or take by force, the necessary food or medicine, or to kidnap, and compel to officiate, the only qualified medical practitioner." Mill commented on this passage in his letter to E. W. Young (1867, CW vol. XVI, pp. 1327–28):

> I do not claim any greater latitude of making exceptions to general rules of morality on the utilitarian theory than is accorded by moralists on all theories. Every ethical system admits the possibility & even frequency, of a conflict of duties. In most cases the conflict occasions no great difficulty, because one of the duties is in general obviously paramount to the other. The difficulty arises when the choice is between a very great violation of a duty usually subordinate & a very small infringement of one ordinarily of more peremptory obligation. In such a case the former, I cannot but think, may be the greater moral offence. When I mentioned, as a case of this kind, the case of stealing or taking by force the food or medicine necessary for saving a life, I was thinking rather of saving another person's life than one's own. A much stricter rule is required in the latter case than in the former, for the obvious reason, that there is more probability of self deception or of dishonesty. But I am far from saying that the rule sh^d

never be relaxed even when the case is one's own. A runaway slave by the laws of slave countries commits a theft: he steals his own person from his lawful owner. If you say, this is not morally theft, because property in a human being ought not to exist, take the case of a child or an apprentice who runs away on account of intolerable ill usage. There is in the doctrine I maintain nothing inconsistent with the loftiest estimation of the heroism of martyrs. There are times when the grandest results for the human race depend on [p. 1328] the public assertion of one's convictions at the risk of death by torture. When this is the case martyrdom may be a duty; & in cases when it does not become the duty of all it may be an admirable act of virtue in whoever does it, & a duty in those who as leaders or teachers are bound to set an example of virtue to others, & to do more for the common faith or cause than a simple believer. I do not know whether what I have written will do anything towards removing your difficulty, but I have not leisure to enter further into the subject.

For more of Mill's remarks on the topic of breaking rules in exceptional circumstances, see Appendix A.

Appendix A: Breaking Rules in Exceptional Circumstances

Some passages in *Utilitarianism* (particularly in paragraphs II.23, II.25, and V.37) suggest that in exceptional circumstances, normally binding rules ought to be broken. This view is also reflected in the following remarks, and is of particular interest as complicating the prospect of interpreting Mill as advocating (what has been called since the middle of the twentieth century) rule utilitarianism.

a. From "Sedgwick's Discourse" (1835, CW vol. X, p. 72):

> If utility be the standard, "the end," in the Professor's opinion, "will be made to sanctify the means" [. . .]. We answer— just so far as in any other system, and no farther. In every system of morality, the end, when good, justifies all means which do not conflict with some more important good. On Mr. Sedgwick's own scheme, are there not ends which sanctify actions, in other cases deserving the utmost abhorrence— such, for instance, as taking the life of a fellow-creature in cold blood, in the face of the whole people? According to the principle of utility, the end justifies all means necessary to its attainment, except those which are more mischievous than the end is useful; an exception amply sufficient.

b. From "Taylor's Statesman" (1837, CW vol. XIX, pp. 638–40):

> To admit the balance of consequences as a test of right and wrong, necessarily implies the possibility of exceptions to any derivative rule of morality which may be deduced from that test. If evil will arise in any specific case from our telling truth, we are forbidden by a law of morality from doing that evil: we are forbidden by another law of morality from telling falsehood. Here then are two laws of morality in conflict, and we cannot satisfy both of them. What is to be done but to resort to the primary test of all right and wrong, and to make a specific calculation of the good or evil consequences, as fully and impartially as we [p. 639] can? The evil of departing from a

well-known and salutary rule is indeed one momentous item on that side of the account; but to treat it as equal to infinity, and as necessarily superseding the measurement of any finite quantities of evil on the opposite side, appears to us to be the most fatal of all mistakes in ethical theory.

[...]

It seems to us that all the reasons by which Mr. Taylor establishes the necessity of recognising exceptional cases to general rules of morality in public life are no less applicable to prove the like necessity in private life. [...] [T]he necessity of weighing specific mischief against the evil of departure from a general rule, is in reality the heaviest of all obligations which can possibly be imposed either upon a statesman or upon a private individual; and moral acting would be rendered easier, instead of more difficult, if it could be reduced in every case to a blindfold obedience to some one pre-established [p. 640] rule. Unfortunately this cannot be done, because the moral rules are perpetually liable to clash with one another, and actually do so clash in all those exceptional cases now under consideration, so as to leave us no resource except in a direct appeal to the supreme authority from whence all moral rules are derived.

We know that those who hold this doctrine are accused of licensing immorality, and we admit that the process not only carries with it a serious responsibility, but will be ill performed if there enter into it either bad faith or want of intelligence. But is not the same thing true of the difficult conjunctures in every man's daily walk or profession—in trade, in navigation, in medical practice? And do we really assist a virtuous man in these moral emergencies, by enjoining him to shut his eyes to all the evil on one side of the question? It is rather curious to remark, that the charge against the philosophical moralists, who maintain the necessity of resorting to specific calculation in certain exceptional cases, is the direct reverse of the reproach which is addressed to philosophers in other departments of science. In other sciences, philosophers are censured for attending exclusively to classes, and despising individuals—for looking only to essential qualities, and neglecting altogether what is accidental or particular to the case before them—for a barbarous readiness to inflict any amount of specific evil, if it be necessary in the carrying out of their theories. In moral philosophy, the analytical writers incur the opposite imputation. Because they maintain the necessity of specific calculation in certain exceptional cases, they are treated as if they annihilated all moral rules—as if the individual action was everything, and the class of actions nothing, in their estimation—as if they suffered themselves to be absorbed by that which is accidental and special to the case before them, and were incapable of fully appreciating the more comprehensive considerations on the other side. Philosophy commands that in dealing with any particular case, the whole of the circumstances, without exception, should be taken into view, essential as well as accidental: and if a man wilfully overlooks the latter, when they are pregnant with mischievous consequences, he cannot discharge himself from moral responsibility by pleading that he had the general rule in his favour. What should we say to a physician, who communicated an agonising piece of family intelligence, in reply to the inquiry of our sick friend, at a moment when the slightest aggravation of malady threatened to place him beyond all hope of recovery? In a case like this, surely there is no man of common sense or virtue, who would think for a moment of sheltering himself under the inexorable law of veracity, and refusing to entertain any thought of the irreparable specific mischief on the other side.

c. From "Carlyle's French Revolution" (1837, CW vol. XX, p. 161):

Doubtless, in the infinite complexities of human affairs, any general theorem which a wise man will form concerning them, must be regarded as a mere approximation to truth; an approximation obtained by striking an average of many cases, and consequently not exactly fitting any one case. No wise man, therefore, will stand upon his theorem only—neglecting to look into the specialties of the case in hand, and see what features *that* may present which may take it out of any theorem, or bring it within the compass of more theorems than one. But the far greater number of people—when they have got a formula by rote, when they can bring the matter in hand within some maxim "in that case made and provided" by the traditions of the vulgar, by the doctrines of their sect or school, or by some generalization of their own—do not think it necessary to let their mind's eye rest upon the thing itself at all; but deliberate and act, not upon knowledge of the thing, but upon a hearsay of it; being (to use a frequent illustration of our author) provided with spectacles, they fancy it not needful to use their eyes. It should be understood that general principles are not intended to dispense with thinking and examining, but to help us to think and examine. When the object itself is out of our reach, and we cannot examine into it, we must follow general principles, because, by doing so, we are not so likely to go wrong, and almost certain not to go so far wrong, as if we floated on the boundless ocean of mere conjecture; but when we are not driven to guess, when we have means and appliances for observing, general principles are nothing more or other than helps towards a better use of those means and appliances.

d.   From *A System of Logic* (1843, CW vol. VIII, pp. 943–46):

In all branches of practical business, there are cases in which individuals are bound to conform their practice to a pre-established rule, while [p. 944] there are others in which it is part of their task to find or construct the rule by which they are to govern their conduct. The first, for example, is the case of a judge, under a definite written code. The judge is not called upon to determine what course would be intrinsically the most advisable in the particular case in hand, but only within what rule of law it falls; what the legislature has ordained to be done in the kind of case, and must therefore be presumed to have intended in the individual case. [. . .]

In order that our illustration of the opposite case may be taken from the same class of subjects as the former, we will suppose, in contrast with the situation of the judge, the position of the legislator. As the judge has laws for his guidance, so the legislator has rules, and maxims of policy; but it would be a manifest error to suppose that the legislator is bound

by these maxims in the same manner as the judge is bound
by the laws, and that all he has to do is to argue down from
them to the particular case, as the judge does from the laws.
The legislator is bound to take into consideration the reasons
or grounds of the maxim; the judge has nothing to do with
those of the law, except so far as a consideration of them
may throw light upon the intention of the law-maker, where
his words have left it doubtful. To the judge, the rule, once
positively ascertained, is final; but the legislator, or other
practitioner, who goes by rules rather than by their reasons,
like the old-fashioned German tacticians who were van-
quished by Napoleon, or the physician who preferred that
his patients should die by rule rather than recover contrary to
it, is rightly judged to be a mere pedant, and the slave of his
formulas.

[. . .]

[p. 945]

[. . .] in the complicated affairs of life, and still more in
those of states and societies, rules cannot be relied on, without
constantly referring back to the scientific laws on which they
are founded. To know what are the practical contingencies
which require a modification [p. 946] of the rule, or which
are altogether exceptions to it, is to know what combinations
of circumstances would interfere with, or entirely counteract,
the consequences of those laws: and this can only be learnt by
a reference to the theoretic grounds of the rule.

By a wise practitioner, therefore, rules of conduct will
only be considered as provisional. Being made for the most
numerous cases, or for those of most ordinary occurrence,
they point out the manner in which it will be least peril-
ous to act, where time or means do not exist for analysing
the actual circumstances of the case, or where we cannot
trust our judgment in estimating them. But they do not at
all supersede the propriety of going through (when circumstances permit) the scientific process requisite for framing
a rule from the data of the particular case before us. At the
same time, the common rule may very properly serve as an
admonition that a certain mode of action has been found by
ourselves and others to be well adapted to the cases of most

common occurrence; so that if it be unsuitable to the case in hand, the reason of its being so will be likely to arise from some unusual circumstance.

The error is therefore apparent, of those who would deduce the line of conduct proper to particular cases, from supposed universal practical maxims; overlooking the necessity of constantly referring back to the principles of the speculative science, in order to be sure of attaining even the specific end which the rules have in view. How much greater still, then, must the error be, of setting up such unbending principles, not merely as universal rules for attaining a given end, but as rules of conduct generally [. . .].

e. From "Whewell on Moral Philosophy" (1852, CW vol. X, p. 182):

[. . .] the admission of exceptions to rules is a necessity equally felt in all systems of morality. To take an obvious instance, the rule against homicide, the rule against deceiving, the rule against taking advantage of superior physical strength, and various other important moral rules, are suspended against enemies in the field, and partially against malefactors in private life: in each case suspended as far as is required by the peculiar nature of the case. That the moralities arising from the special circumstances of the action may be so important as to overrule those arising from the class of acts to which it belongs, perhaps to take it out of the category of virtues into that of crimes, or *vice versâ*, is a liability common to all ethical systems.

f. See the excerpt from Mill's letter to E. W. Young (1867) in note 4 of Chapter V.

g. From *The Subjection of Women* (1869, CW vol. XXI, p. 307):

[. . .] women are comparatively unlikely to fall into the common error of men, that of sticking to their rules in a case whose specialities either take it out of the class to which the rules are applicable, or require a special adaptation of them.

h.   From "Thornton on Labour and Its Claims" (1869, CW
     vol. V, p. 659):

[. . .] we have a fresh proof how little even the most plausible of
these absolute maxims of right and wrong are to be depended
on, and how unsafe it is to lose sight, even for a moment, of
the paramount principle—the good of the human race. The
maxims may, as the rough results of experience, be regarded
as *primâ facie* presumptions that what they inculcate will be
found conducive to the ultimate end; but not as conclusive
on that point without examination, still less as carrying an
authority independent of, and superior to, the end.

i.   From "Berkeley's Life and Writings" (1871, CW vol. XI,
     pp. 468–69):

In his writings on practical subjects there is much to commend, and a good deal to criticise. One of them is a vindication of *Passive Obedience, or the Christian doctrine of not resisting the Supreme Power.* It is an impressive lesson of tolerance,
to find so great a man as Berkeley a thoroughly convinced
adherent and defender of a doctrine not only so pernicious,
but by that time so thoroughly gone by. The reader of the
tract perceives that the writer was misled by an exaggerated
application of that cardinal doctrine of morality, the importance of general rules. As it was acknowledged that the cases
in which it is right to disobey the laws or rebel against the
Government are not the rule but the exception, Berkeley
threw [p. 469] them out altogether, for his moral rules admitted of no exceptions.

Appendix B: Maximization and Supererogation

In paragraph V.14, Mill refers to "the distinction between morality and simple expediency." Various other passages in *Utilitarianism* also suggest that producing as much happiness as possible is not always obligatory, though it may of course still be commendable—that is, that producing as much happiness as possible may be supererogatory. This view is of particular interest as complicating the prospect of interpreting Mill as advocating (what has been called since the middle of the twentieth century) act utilitarianism. For more on this topic, see the following remarks:

a. From *On Liberty* (1859, CW vol. XVIII, p. 279 and pp. 281–82):

[. . .] the self-regarding faults previously mentioned [. . .] are not properly immoralities, and to whatever pitch they may be carried, do not constitute wickedness. They may be proofs of any amount of folly, or want of personal dignity and self-respect; but they are only a subject of moral reprobation when they involve a breach of duty to others, for whose sake the individual is bound to have care for himself. What are called duties to ourselves are not socially obligatory, unless circumstances render them at the same time duties to others. The term duty to oneself, when it means anything more than prudence, means self-respect or self-development; and for none of these is any one accountable to his fellow creatures, because for none of them is it for the good of mankind that he be held accountable to them.

[. . .]

[p. 281]

[. . .]

I fully admit that the mischief which a person does to himself may seriously affect, both through their sympathies and their interests, those nearly connected with him, and in a minor degree, society at large. When, by conduct of this sort, a person is led to violate a distinct and assignable obligation to any other person or persons, the case is taken out of the

self-regarding class, and becomes amenable to moral disapprobation in the proper sense of the term. If, for example, a
man, through intemperance or extravagance, becomes unable
to pay his debts, or, having undertaken the moral responsibility of a family, becomes from the same cause incapable of sup-
porting or educating them, he is deservedly reprobated, and
might be justly punished: but it is for the breach of duty to his
family or creditors, not for the extravagance. If the resources
which ought to have been devoted to them, had been diverted
from them for the most prudent investment, the moral culpa-
bility would have been the same. George Barnwell murdered
his uncle to get money for his mistress, but if he had done
it to set himself up in business, he would equally have been
hanged. Again, in the frequent case of a man who causes grief
to his family by addiction to bad habits, he deserves reproach
for his unkindness or ingratitude; but so he may for cultivating habits not in themselves vicious, if they are painful to
those with whom he passes his life, or who from personal ties
are dependent on him for their comfort. Whoever fails in the
consideration generally due to the interests and feelings of
others, not being compelled by some more imperative duty,
or justified by allowable self-preference, is a subject of moral
disapprobation for that failure, but not for the cause of it, nor
for the errors, merely personal to himself, which may have
remotely led to it. In like [p. 282] manner, when a person
disables himself, by conduct purely self-regarding, from the
performance of some definite duty incumbent on him to the
public, he is guilty of a social offence. No person ought to
be punished simply for being drunk; but a soldier or a police-
man should be punished for being drunk on duty. Whenever,
in short, there is a definite damage, or a definite risk of damage,
either to an individual or to the public, the case is taken out of
the province of liberty, and placed in that of morality or law.

b.   From Mill's letter to George Grote (1862, CW vol. XV, p. 762):

[. . .] general rules must be laid down for people's conduct to
one another, or in other words, rights and obligations must, as
you say, be recognised; and people must, on the one hand, not

be required to sacrifice even their own less good to another's greater, where no general rule has given the other a right to the sacrifice; while, when a right *has* been recognised, they must, in most cases, yield to that right even at the sacrifice, in the particular case, of their own greater good to another's less. [. . .] These, I think, are exactly your conclusions. And they are consistent with recognising the merit, though not the duty, of making still greater sacrifices of our own less good to the greater good of others, than the general conditions of human happiness render it expedient to prescribe.

c.   From *Auguste Comte and Positivism* (1865, CW vol. X, pp. 337–38):

The most prejudiced must admit that this religion without theology [i.e., Comte's view] is not chargeable with relaxation of moral restraints. On the contrary, it prodigiously exaggerates them. It makes the same ethical mistake as the theory of Calvinism, that every act in life should be done for the glory of God, and that whatever is not a duty is a sin. It does not perceive that between the region of duty and that of sin there is an intermediate space, the region of positive worthiness. It is not good that persons should be bound, by other people's opinion, to do everything that they would deserve praise for doing. There is a standard of altruism to which all should be required to come up, and a degree beyond it which is not obligatory, but meritorious. It is incumbent on every one to restrain the pursuit of his personal objects within the limits consistent with the essential interests of others. What those limits are, it is the province of ethical science to determine; and to keep all individuals and aggregations of individuals within them, is the proper office of punishment and of moral blame. If in addition to fulfilling this obligation, persons [p. 338] make the good of others a direct object of disinterested exertions, postponing or sacrificing to it even innocent personal indulgences, they deserve gratitude and honour, and are fit objects of moral praise. So long as they are in no way compelled to this conduct by any external pressure, there cannot be too much of it; but a necessary condition is its spontaneity; since the notion of a happiness for all, procured by the self-sacrifice of each, if the abnegation is really felt to be a sacrifice, is a contradiction. Such spontaneity by no means excludes sympathetic encouragement; but the encouragement should take the form of making self-devotion pleasant, not that of making everything else painful. The object should be to stimulate services to humanity by their natural rewards; not to render the pursuit of our own good in any other manner impossible, by visiting it with the reproaches of other and of our own conscience. The proper office of those sanctions is to enforce upon every one, the conduct necessary to give all other persons their fair chance: conduct which chiefly consists in not doing them harm, and not impeding them in anything which without harming others does good to themselves. To this must of course be added, that when we either expressly or tacitly undertake to do more, we are bound to keep our promise. And inasmuch as every one, who avails himself of the advantages of society, leads others to expect from him all such positive good offices and disinterested services as the moral improvement attained by mankind has rendered customary, he deserves moral blame if, without just cause, he disappoints that expectation. Through this principle the domain of moral duty, in an improving society, is always widening. When what once was uncommon virtue becomes common virtue, it comes to be numbered among obligations, while a degree exceeding what has grown common, remains simply meritorious.

d.   From Mill's letter to Henry S. Brandreth (1867, CW vol. XVI, p. 1234):

There are cases in which martyrdom is a useless self sacrifice, & a sacrifice of other means of doing real good. There are other cases in which the importance of it to the good of mankind is so great as to make it a positive duty, like the act of a soldier who gives his life in the performance of what is assigned to him. There are cases again where without being so necessary as to be, on the utilitarian ground, an absolute duty, it is yet so useful as to constitute an act of virtue, which then ought to receive the praise & honours of heroism.

e. From "Thornton on Labour and Its Claims" (1869, CW vol. V, pp. 650–51):

Utilitarian morality fully recognises the distinction between the province of positive duty and that of virtue, but maintains that the standard and rule of both is the general interest. From the utilitarian point of view, the distinction between them is the following:—There are many acts, and a still greater number of [p. 651] forbearances, the perpetual practice of which by all is so necessary to the general well-being, that people must be held to it compulsorily, either by law, or by social pressure. These acts and forbearances constitute duty. Outside these bounds there is the innumerable variety of modes in which the acts of human beings are either a cause, or a hindrance, of good to their fellow-creatures, but in regard to which it is, on the whole, for the general interest that they should be left free; being merely encouraged, by praise and honour, to the performance of such beneficial actions as are not sufficiently stimulated by benefits flowing from them to the agent himself. This larger sphere is that of Merit or Virtue.

Appendix C: The Art of Life

In the last sentence of paragraph II.10, Mill distinguishes between "the end of human action" and "the standard of morality." In paragraph V.14, Mill refers to "the distinction between morality and simple expediency." In these remarks, Mill seems to be alluding to his doctrine of the Art of Life. Two earlier works contain remarks developing this doctrine more explicitly.

    a.   From "Bentham" (1838, CW vol. X, pp. 112–13):

> He [Bentham] is chargeable also with another error, which it would be improper to pass over, because nothing has tended more to place him in opposition to the common feelings of mankind, and to give to his philosophy that cold, mechanical, and ungenial air which characterizes the popular idea of a Benthamite. This error, or rather one-sidedness, belongs to him not as a utilitarian, but as a moralist by profession, and in common with almost all professed moralists, whether religious or philosophical: it is that of treating the *moral* view of actions and characters, which is unquestionably the first and most important mode of looking at them, as if it were the sole one: whereas it is only one of three, by all of which our sentiments towards the human being may be, ought to be, and without entirely crushing our own nature cannot but be, materially influenced. Every human action has three aspects: its *moral* aspect, or that of its *right* and *wrong*; its *æsthetic* aspect, or that of its *beauty*; its *sympathetic* aspect, or that of its *loveableness*. The first addresses itself to our reason and conscience; the second to our imagination; the third to our human fellow-feeling. According to the first, we approve or disapprove; according to the second, we admire or despise; according to the third, we love, pity, or dislike. The morality of an action depends on its foreseeable consequences; its beauty, and its loveableness, or the reverse, depend on the qualities which it is evidence of. Thus, a lie is *wrong*, because its effect is to mislead, and because it tends to destroy the confidence of man in man; it is also *mean*, because it is cowardly—because it proceeds from not daring to face the consequences of telling the

truth—or at best is evidence of want of that *power* to compass our ends by straightforward means, which is conceived as
properly belonging to every person not deficient in energy or
in understanding. The action of Brutus in sentencing his sons
was *right*, because it was executing a law essential to the freedom of his country, against persons of whose guilt there was
no doubt: it was *admirable*, because it evinced a rare degree
of patriotism, courage, and self-control; but there was nothing *loveable* in it; it affords either no presumption in regard
to loveable qualities, or a presumption of their deficiency. If
one of the sons had engaged in the conspiracy from affection for the other, his action would [p. 113] have been loveable, though neither moral nor admirable. It is not possible for
any sophistry to confound these three modes of viewing an
action; but it is very possible to adhere to one of them exclusively, and lose sight of the rest.

b.   From the first and second editions of *A System of Logic*
     (1843 and 1846, CW vol. VIII, p. 943):

[. . .] ethics, or morality, is properly a portion of the art corresponding to the sciences of human nature and society: the
remainder consisting of prudence or policy, and the art of
education.

c.   From sections that Mill added to the third edition (and
     retained in all subsequent editions) of *A System of Logic*
     (1851, CW vol. VIII, pp. 949–51):

But though the reasonings which connect the end or purpose of every art with its means, belong to the domain of
Science, the definition of the end itself belongs exclusively
to Art, and forms its peculiar province. Every art has one first
principle, or general major premise, not borrowed from science; that which enunciates the object aimed at, and affirms
it to be a desirable object. The builder's art assumes that it is
desirable to have buildings; architecture (as one of the fine arts),
that it is desirable to have them beautiful or imposing. The
hygienic and medical arts assume, the one that the preservation

of health, the other that the cure of disease, are fitting and desirable ends. [. . .] [T]here is need of general premises, determining what are the proper objects of approbation, and what the proper order of precedence among those objects.

These general premises, together with the principal conclusions which may be deduced from them, form (or rather might form) a body of doctrine, which is properly the Art of Life, in its three departments, Morality, Prudence or Policy, and Æsthetics; the Right, the Expedient, and the Beautiful or Noble, in human conduct and works. To this art, (which, in the main, is unfortunately still to be created,) all other arts are subordinate; since its principles are those which must determine whether the special aim of any particular art is worthy and desirable, and what is its place in the scale of desirable things. Every art is thus a joint result of laws of nature disclosed by science, and of the general principles of what has been called Teleology, or the Doctrine of Ends; which, borrowing the language of the German meta- [p. 950] physicians, may also be termed, not improperly, the principles of Practical Reason.

[. . .]

[p. 951]

[. . .]

The theory of the foundations of morality is a subject which it would be out of place, in a work like this, to discuss at large, and which could not to any useful purpose be treated incidentally. I shall content myself therefore with saying, that the doctrine of intuitive moral principles, even if true, would provide only for that portion of the field of conduct which is properly called moral. For the remainder of the practice of life some general principle, or standard, must still be sought; and if that principle be rightly chosen, it will be found, I apprehend, to serve quite as well for the ultimate principle of Morality, as for that of Prudence, Policy, or Taste.

Without attempting in this place to justify my opinion, or even to define the kind of justification which it admits of, I merely declare my conviction, that the general principle to which all rules of practice ought to conform, and the test by which they should be tried, is that of conduciveness to the happiness of mankind, or rather, of all sentient beings: in other words, that the promotion of happiness is the ultimate principle of Teleology.

The 1865 edition of *A System of Logic* had the following footnote attached to the last sentence:

For an express discussion and vindication of this principle, see the little volume entitled *Utilitarianism*.